Mathematical Models

in the

Social Sciences

MATHEMATICAL MODELS

IN THE

SOCIAL SCIENCES

John G. Kemeny

J. Laurie Snell

The MIT Press
Cambridge, Massachusetts, and London, England

Original edition published by Blaisdell Publishing Company,
a division of Ginn and Company

Copyright © 1962 by Ginn and Company

Copyright transferred to The Massachusetts Institute of Technology, 1972

First MIT Press edition, July 1972
Second printing, February 1973

Printed and bound in the United States of America

Library of Congress Cataloging in Publication Data

Kemeny, John G
    Mathematical models in the social sciences.

    Reprint of the 1962 ed., issued in series:
Introductions to higher mathematics.
    Bibliography: p.
    1. Social sciences—Mathematical models.
I. Snell, James Laurie, joint author. II. Title.
[H61.K43 1972]   300'.1'51   72–4880
ISBN 0–262–11047–4

Preface

This book is based on notes developed for a one semester junior mathematics course at Dartmouth College. The course is a natural counterpart of the usual "Mathematical Methods of Physics" course, with techniques and applications selected from the social sciences. Since the course is frequently elected by social science majors, the prerequisites have been kept at a minimum.

It should be emphasized that this book is designed for a mathematics course, not for a course in the social sciences. The subject matter to be taught is mathematical; the problems in the social sciences are introduced only to provide motivation for learning certain techniques. In this sense, the analogy to the courses in "Mathematical Methods of Physics" is complete.

Chapter I is designed to give background information on the nature of mathematical models, and to serve as a methodological guide for the remaining chapters. It is hoped that the student will read this chapter first, and that he will return to it periodically as he progresses through the rest of the volume.

The remaining chapters are independent of each other.* The instructor may select any subset of the models for his course. Our experience indicates that a semester course can conveniently cover five or six models. Each chapter will formulate one or more problems both from the point of view of the social scientist and of the mathematician. The major part of the chapter is devoted to teaching the student the necessary mathematical techniques, and in applying them to the stated problems. Finally the results are interpreted.

The prerequisites for the course at Dartmouth consist of a year of calculus and a course in finite mathematics.† The student should be acquainted with the basic techniques of differentiating and integrating functions of one variable, and should know how to solve a very simple differential equation. In addition some elementary knowledge of probability theory and of matrix methods is assumed.

In some cases it was convenient to make use of techniques which go beyond these prerequisites; these are treated in the appendices. In each

---

* Except that Chapter IV should follow Chapter III.

† Based on John G. Kemeny, J. Laurie Snell, and G. L. Thompson, *Introduction to Finite Mathematics* (Englewood Cliffs, N. J.: Prentice-Hall, 1957), ch. I–V; or on John G. Kemeny and others, *Finite Mathematical Structures* (Englewood Cliffs, N. J.: Prentice-Hall, 1959), ch. 1–4.

case only a rudimentary knowledge of these more advanced methods is
needed.

It is hoped that the course will not only offer a new, attractive elective
for mathematics majors, but that it can form part of a two-year mathematics sequence for social science students. A year of calculus, followed by
a semester of finite mathematics, followed by a course based on the present
volume, should meet the minimum standards recommended for social
scientists desiring to do theoretical work.

Each chapter (other than Chapter I) contains a list of exercises of varying
difficulty, and suggested projects in which the student may exercise his
creative ability. Several of these projects are designed to encourage the
student to develop his own model, and it is hoped that better students
would wish to do this to the degree of detail illustrated in the present
volume. A short list of references has also been included in most of the
chapters, which will, among other things, contain the works which are
informally mentioned in the text.

The authors wish to express their thanks to S. Grossberg, M. W. Herriott,
W. E. Marsh, and M. R. Schwartz, who—as undergraduate research
assistants—contributed much to the preparation of the present volume.
They also wish to thank Mrs. Margaret Andrews, Mrs. Helen Hanchett,
and Mrs. Delia Pillsbury for their patient help in preparing the manuscript.
The authors are also indebted to the Dartmouth College Computation
Center for computing many examples.

John G. Kemeny

J. Laurie Snell

Hanover, New Hampshire

Contents

Mathematical Models

in the

Social Sciences

CHAPTER I

On the Methodology of Mathematical Models

To understand the role played by mathematical models in science we must first have some understanding of the nature of the scientific method. The scientific method may initially be described as a cyclic process through which human beings learn from experience. As evidence accumulates, theories in better and better agreement with the actual functioning of nature can be formulated.

The basic cycle of the scientific method may be divided into three steps: induction, deduction, and verification. *Induction* is the step which carries the scientist from factual observations to the formation of theories. These theories may be very close to facts in that they "simply summarize observed facts," or they may be as abstract as are those of modern theoretical physics. The inductive step is necessarily creative, and, although various rules to aid the theoretical scientist have been proposed, these are at best uncertain guides and not by any means guarantees of success. The scientist is able to investigate a process under only a small number of conditions, after which he must attempt to explain it in its complete generality. Thus, even an inspired theory is in part an inspired guess.

Once the theory is formulated precisely, the tools of logic and mathematics are available to deduce consequences from it. It is due to the availability of the second, deductive, step that the formation of theories becomes of importance to the scientist. For it is during the process of *deduction* that the scientist discovers a number of consequences of his theories which may not have been immediately obvious to him. In some cases the chain of deduction may take many years, and the results may be quite unexpected.

Once a number of interesting consequences have been deduced from the theory, they must be put to the test of experimental *verification*. In some cases the newly deduced facts may correspond to events already observed, whereas in other instances new observations and experiments will be required to test the predictions. In the former case one speaks of the theory as having served to explain known facts; in the latter we have succeeded in predicting novel occurrences.

Our confidence in a theory builds up as more and more of its predictions turn out to be true. On the other hand, it happens frequently in the history of science that further testing persuades us to reject a previously accepted

3

theory. Very often the rejection of one theory directly stimulates the formulation of another, improved theory—one which explains both those old facts on which the discarded theory was based and those new facts which have led to the rejection of the old theory.

In this book we consider eight mathematical models illustrating theories from a variety of different branches of the social sciences. Each chapter is organized in a manner paralleling the usual application of the scientific method. First a problem is stated from a branch of the social sciences, then a mathematical model (theory) is formed, then a number of consequences are deduced from this theory, and finally the results are interpreted. We hope that this procedure will illustrate the manner in which theories are formed. Indeed it should illustrate the entire cycle of the scientific method, with the exception of the gathering of facts. That is, we start with a collection of facts already given to us and end at the point where we are ready to put the predictions of our theory to further observational tests.

Although most of our chapters illustrate the basic cycle, the entire cycle can best be observed in Chapter V. After forming a mathematical model for a small-groups experiment and developing it in some detail, we present experimental evidence indicating that the original model may not be adequate, and we show how the very act of disconfirmation suggests an improved model.

It is important to contrast the pure mathematical theory with its interpreted version that serves as a model. Let us illustrate this in terms of the ecology model of Chapter III. From the point of view of pure mathematics, we are confronted with a pair of simple differential equations. These equations are neither true nor false, since they have no factual content. Rather, they are abstract forms which may be studied, and from which we can deduce certain "if ... then ..." statements. For example, we can show that if certain quantities of any sort happen to obey the laws of nature expressed in our equations, then these quantities must forever be on the trajectory determined by their initial values.

Next we find that certain species of animal seem to multiply in a manner that roughly may be considered to obey these differential equations. We thus supply an interpretation, letting x and y stand for actual numbers of the two species and interpreting t as time measured in a convenient unit. We have thereby automatically supplied interpretations for all the results that may be deduced from these equations. Each of these deductions, interpreted in the indicated manner, must either correspond to a known fact or serve as a prediction of an unknown fact.

Closely related to the formation of scientific theories is the problem of how scientists arrive at their basic concepts. Of particular interest are the so-called theoretical concepts, those concepts which are reasonably far removed from terms that describe our immediate experience. The history of science points to the conclusion that the most useful theoretical concepts are formed simultaneously with the most useful theories. That is, the only test of the fruitfulness of a given concept is the fact that we are able to form fruitful theories in its terms. It is therefore not surprising that in most of the following chapters it is difficult to separate the formation of a concept from the formulation of the mathematical model. However, Chapter II comes as close to pure concept formation as one can ever hope to find in a scientific context.

Indeed, in Chapter II the primary problem is not so much that of forming a mathematical model as it is that of developing a mathematical tool (a "distance" between rankings) which may later on be used in building a variety of different models. Such a technique, known as *explication*, is becoming very popular for the formation of precise concepts. One begins with an imprecisely expressed idea and hopefully arrives at a quite precise and fruitful concept. The general procedure is as follows: First one lays down the conditions of adequacy that a precise definition must meet; then one searches out the simplest definition that will meet all of them. Chapter II carries out such a procedure and indicates in some detail the types of problems with which one is confronted in the formation of mathematical concepts.†

Very often one finds that a single vague, intuitive idea leads to a number of distinct and precise concepts, each of which may turn out to be fruitful in different applications. This is well illustrated in terms of our intuitive idea of a structure being "in balance" or "in equilibrium." This idea receives different precise formulations in Chapters III, IV, and VIII, where we discuss the equilibrium or balance of a pair of species, a market, and a political structure, respectively.

Let us now group mathematical models used in the sciences into types. One fundamental distinction is whether or not a model is of a so-called "deterministic" nature. The distinction can be illustrated in terms of classical physics. For example, Newton's laws are of a deterministic nature; i.e., if one has sufficient information available concerning the past, one can predict the entire future of the system. On the other hand the models of statistical mechanics are non-deterministic and therefore probabilistic in nature; that is, no matter how much information one has about the past, one can predict only the probabilities of certain future occurrences, and usually the amount of information available loses its value as time passes. Deterministic models will be found in Chapters III, IV, VI and IX. Probabilistic models are treated in Chapters V and VII. The reader should compare the predictions that one deduces from the two types of models.

† The application of the concept of distance developed in Chapter II was to consensus rankings by a group of experts, which is a procedural matter rather than a scientific theory. However, once such concepts are available, they often prove useful in new contexts. For example, J. Berger is working on a theory of small groups of experiments which makes essential use of this concept of distance.

It should in particular be noted that mere differences in the sorts of predictions that one can hope to make with each type of model do not imply that one sort of prediction is less useful than the other.

All the above-mentioned models share the feature of being "predictive" in nature. They may be contrasted with the models in Chapters II and VIII, which are primarily "descriptive." The model in Chapter II allows us to compare different rankings of the same set of objects, whereas the model in Chapter VIII allows us to classify social structures.

It is sometimes useful to distinguish theories by their levels of abstraction. We may illustrate this distinction either in terms of the deterministic theories or in terms of the probabilistic ones. Chapters III and IV both treat deterministic differential equation models. But the model of Chapter III is much closer to the level of observations. In this ecological model the variables represent directly observable quantities; namely, numbers of animals in various species. In contrast, Chapter IV attempts to describe the "underlying machinery" that operates a market. Such quantities as are needed to describe the utility of various goods for various individuals are not directly observable.

Similarly, of the two probabilistic models, the one in Chapter VII is less abstract than the one in Chapter V. The former deals with such directly observable quantities as the number of customers in a waiting line; the latter attempts to reconstruct the manner in which a subject in an experiment arrives at his decisions. The subject's mental state is not observable in as simple and easy a way as is service time, which is directly measurable. Of course, none of these models achieve the level of abstraction that characterizes theories in modern physics. In some truly abstract models the connection with experience is established only very indirectly, after long chains of deductions. These levels are as yet rarely reached in the social sciences.

One of the best examples of a more abstract model in the social sciences is a model applicable to simple learning experiments that has been developed by W. K. Estes. We do not treat this in the present volume, as it was treated in some detail in a previous book by the present authors.†

Since many scientists seem to be under the impression that the use of mathematics is closely tied to the existence of numerical concepts, or at least of concepts dealing with space, it is significant that two nonnumerical and nongeometrical models are included in our collection. Both Chapters II and VIII employ techniques that a classical mathematician would not have recognized as mathematics, namely, abstract distances (metric spaces) and graph theory. It is thanks to the ever-broadening conception of the nature of mathematics that such models are available to us today. It is entirely possible that the greatest successes in the very complex areas of

† John G. Kemeny and J. Laurie Snell, *Finite Markov Chains* (Princeton, N. J.: D. Van Nostrand Co., 1960), Chap. VII, Sec. 5.

the social sciences will be made possible by nonnumerical models produced by modern mathematics.

Finally let us ask questions concerning the various uses to which mathematical models can be put. As indicated above, the two primary uses lie in explaining known facts and in predicting facts not as yet known. Of course, each of our chapters illustrates both of these tendencies to some extent; for if the models are correctly formed they will explain the facts on which they were built, and if they contain any element of novelty at all they will make predictions concerning the future.

We will examine one clear-cut example of each type of use of a model. Let us first refer to Chapter III as an example of clear-cut scientific explanation: A cyclic pattern has been observed in the numbers of animals in certain species in closed ecological systems. The simple model developed in the chapter offers an elementary explanation for this cyclic behavior.

A good example of predicting the future is provided by Chapter VII. The "second problem" treated in this chapter has received highly detailed and extensive study because it enables various industries to predict their needs for staff and equipment. For example, it is through methods illustrated in this chapter that the Bell Telephone Company has planned the number and type of trunk lines that it must make available to furnish adequate service to its customers. It is the task of the model to predict how long the average customer will have to wait until a telephone trunk line becomes free, given information concerning the telephone habits of the customers and specifications as to the number of available trunk lines. By carrying out a number of such computations, the company may find the minimum number of trunk lines with which it can furnish what its directorate considers satisfactory service.

The previous example illustrates the fact that, although some predictions are made purely out of scientific curiosity, in many instances models with strong predictive powers may be used as planning devices. This feature is also well illustrated in Chapters VI and IX. The technique discussed in the latter chapter, dynamic programming, has in the last fifteen years proven invaluable as a planning device for industry. The former chapter contains a novel idea, suggested as a planning device for the first time in this book.

We hope that one by-product of the present book will be a reinforcement of the general impression that mathematics has broad and fruitful applications. Although this point has been conceded in the physical sciences, and to some extent in the biological sciences, there are still many skeptics as far as the social sciences are concerned. To some extent this skepticism is due to the very legitimate objection that the social sciences are vastly more complex than the physical or biological sciences. However, this seems to indicate only that their mathematical techniques will have to be more sophisticated as well. It also indicates that the time which it will take to develop nontrivial models for the social sciences may have to be substantial, even in the present age of rapid scientific progress.

But to some extent the objections are based on a misunderstanding of the nature of mathematics. Mathematics is best viewed as the study of abstract relations in the broadest sense of that word. From this point of view it is not surprising that mathematics is applicable to any well-defined field. Whatever the nature of the phenomena studied in a given social science, their various components do bear certain relations to each other, and once one succeeds in formulating these abstractly and precisely, one is in a position to apply the full machinery of mathematical analysis. Of course, it is to be expected that often the mathematical model so formed will be one not previously studied by mathematicians. Therefore, one may look forward to the day when the social sciences will be as major a stimulus for the development of new mathematics as physics has been in the past.

On the other hand, it has been the good luck of both science and mathematics that mathematical models which were developed by mathematicians purely for their aesthetic satisfaction have subsequently proved to be extremely useful. An outstanding example of this in the physical sciences was the invention of "imaginary numbers," which, as their very name indicates, were supposed to have no connection with reality. As it has turned out, however, these numbers play a crucial role in modern physics. For example, all of electromagnetic theory is based on their use.

It is not even too surprising to find that the same abstract mathematical model may serve a variety of different purposes. We find good illustrations of this point in two of our chapters. In Chapter VII the same mathematical model is applied on the one hand to the growth of a population, and on the other to the problem of people waiting in line to be served. An even more spectacular illustration of this type of strange coincidence may be found in Chapter VI. The mathematical tools used there were developed by pure mathematicians who were interested in giving a probabilistic generalization of some results from the theory of potentials in classical physics. That these results should turn out to be applicable also to practical planning problems in economics indicates the tremendous flexibility of an abstract model.

REFERENCES

Danto, A., and Morgenbesser, S. *Philosophy of Science.* New York: Meridian Books, 1960.

Feigl, H., and Brodbeck, M. *Readings in the Philosophy of Science.* New York: Appleton-Century-Crofts, 1953.

Kemeny, John G. *A Philosopher Looks at Science.* Princeton: D. Van Nostrand Co., 1959.

Popper, Karl R. *The Logic of Scientific Discovery.* New York: Basic Books, 1959.

Wiener, P. P. *Readings in the Philosophy of Science.* New York: Charles Scribner's Sons, 1953.

CHAPTER II

Preference Rankings
An Axiomatic Approach

1. The problem. Let us consider the problem of ranking a set of objects. Suppose that ten experts are each asked to rank a set of 50 objects in order of preference. To allow a maximum amount of freedom, we will allow ties in the rankings. We are then supposed to arrive at a consensus ranking. How are we to do this?

This problem can be reduced to one which is analogous to those of classical statistics if we are able to introduce a measure of distance between rankings. So, our problem is that of taking the set of all possible rankings of 50 objects and of turning this set into a geometrical space, one on which a definite distance is defined between any two rankings.

Let us agree on some notation. We shall have in mind a fixed number of objects to be ranked. We shall denote possible rankings by the small capital letters A, B, C. For example, if we have three objects a, b, c, in mind, then A may be the ranking where b is first, a is second, and c is third; and B may be the ranking where c is first and a and b are tied for second place. We use the self-explanatory notation:

$$\text{A} = \begin{pmatrix} b \\ a \\ c \end{pmatrix}, \quad \text{B} = \begin{pmatrix} c \\ a\text{–}b \end{pmatrix}.$$

We want to introduce a measure of distance between pairs A and B, which will be denoted by $d(\text{A},\text{B})$. Let us try to agree on certain conditions that such a definition must satisfy. First of all, d must satisfy the conditions for a distance laid down by a geometer. That is:

AXIOM 1.1. $d(\text{A},\text{B}) \geq 0$, *and equality holds if and only if* A *and* B *are the same ranking.*

AXIOM 1.2. $d(\text{A},\text{B}) = d(\text{B},\text{A})$.

AXIOM 1.3. $d(\text{A},\text{B}) + d(\text{B},\text{C}) \geq d(\text{A},\text{C})$, *and the equality holds if and only if the ranking* B *is between* A *and* C.

For Axiom 1.3 we need a definition of "betweenness." We shall define betweenness in terms of pairwise judgments—that is, we shall say that ranking B is *between* A and C if for each pair of objects i and j, the judgment of B is between that of A and C. In other words, for the given pair, the judgment of B either agrees with A or agrees with C, or A prefers i, C prefers j, and B declares them to be tied.

Next, we must assure that our measure of distance does not in any way depend on the particular objects we have chosen for our rankings; that is, the definition of the distance d should not be affected by a relabeling of the set of objects to be ranked.

This means, for example, that if

$$A = \begin{pmatrix} a \\ b \\ c \end{pmatrix}, \quad B = \begin{pmatrix} c \\ b \\ a \end{pmatrix},$$

and if

$$A' = \begin{pmatrix} b \\ c \\ a \end{pmatrix}, \quad B' = \begin{pmatrix} a \\ c \\ b \end{pmatrix},$$

then $d(A,B) = d(A',B')$, since A' and B' may be obtained from A and B by changing a to b, b to c, and c to a. This leads to:

AXIOM 2. *If A' results from A by a permutation of the objects, and B' results from B by the same permutation, then $d(A',B') = d(A,B)$.*

Next we require that if the two rankings are in complete agreement at the beginning of the list and at the end of the list, and differ only as to the ranking of k objects in the middle, then this distance is the same as if these k objects were the only objects under consideration.

This condition is self-explanatory; to make it mathematically precise, we introduce the term *segment*. A set of objects S forms a segment of a given ranking if $C(S)$ (the complement of S) is not empty and if every element in $C(S)$ is either ahead of every element of S or behind every element of S. Then we have:

AXIOM 3. *If two rankings A and B agree except for a set S of k elements, which is a segment of both, then $d(A,B)$ may be computed as if these k objects were the only objects being ranked.*

Our final condition is in the nature of a convention. It may be thought of as choosing a unit of measurement:

AXIOM 4. *The minimum positive distance is 1.*

Let us suppose that we have agreed that these are four reasonable conditions for the definition of a distance between rankings. We have then translated our scientific problem into a purely mathematical problem; hence, we can use purely deductive methods from now on. We can ask a mathematician three questions: (1) Is there any distance that will satisfy all of these conditions? In other words, are our conditions consistent? (2) How can we characterize all definitions that will satisfy these four conditions? (3) What additional assumptions can we make that will narrow the possible choice from many distances to one?

2. Mathematical representation of rankings. The following model has the attractive feature that its mathematical treatment requires only elementary techniques, combined with some common sense.

Our first task is to introduce a convenient representation for a ranking of n objects. (For purposes of illustration we shall usually choose $n = 3$.) We represent the ranking A by a square array of numbers, or a *matrix*, $A = (a_{ij})$, where $i,j = 1, 2, \ldots, n$. We use the convention

$$a_{ij} = \begin{cases} 1 \text{ if } i \text{ is preferred to } j, \\ -1 \text{ if } j \text{ is preferred to } i, \\ 0 \text{ if they are tied.} \end{cases}$$

For example, the ranking $\begin{pmatrix} b \\ a-c \end{pmatrix}$ is represented by

$$\begin{array}{c} \\ a \\ b \\ c \end{array} \begin{array}{ccc} a & b & c \\ \begin{pmatrix} 0 & -1 & 0 \\ 1 & 0 & 1 \\ 0 & -1 & 0 \end{pmatrix} \end{array}.$$

Clearly, any ranking can be represented by such a matrix, but the matrix must be of a special form in order to represent a ranking. The special requirements correspond to the properties of rankings.

To find these conditions we must clarify the nature of rankings. The relationship $a_{ij} = +1$ expresses that i is preferred to j. Such a *preference relation* must be asymmetric and transitive. Hence,

(1) If $a_{ij} = +1$, then $a_{ji} = -1$.

(2) If $a_{ij} = +1$, and $a_{jk} = +1$, then $a_{ik} = +1$.

The relationship $a_{ij} = 0$ expresses that i and j are tied. Such an *equivalence relation* must be reflexive, symmetric, and transitive. That is,

(3) $a_{ii} = 0$.

(4) If $a_{ij} = 0$, then $a_{ji} = 0$.

(5) If $a_{ij} = 0$, and $a_{jk} = 0$, then $a_{ik} = 0$.

The two relations just discussed must be *consistent*, i.e.,

(6) If $a_{ij} = +1$ and $a_{jk} = 0$, then $a_{ik} = +1$.

(7) If $a_{ij} = 0$ and $a_{jk} = +1$, then $a_{ik} = +1$.

Finally our ranking must be *connected*, that is,

(8) For every i and j, $a_{ij} = +1$, or $a_{ji} = +1$, or $a_{ij} = 0$.

So far we have simply summarized what is meant by a ranking. But these eight conditions can be expressed much more simply as follows (see Exercise 1):

(I) $a_{ij} = +1, 0, or -1$.

(II) $a_{ij} = -a_{ji}$.

(III) *If $a_{ij} \geq 0$ and $a_{jk} \geq 0$, then $a_{ik} \geq 0$; and $a_{ik} = 0$ only if both the others are 0.*

We shall refer to matrices with properties (I) through (III) as *ordering matrices*.

Of course this representation leaves a great deal of arbitrariness. We may number our n objects in any order we like. A natural ordering of the objects is according to the ordering A under consideration (with an arbitrary order for tied objects). If we choose such an order, we shall say that the matrix is in a *canonical form*. In our example at the beginning of this section, we would put object b first, and then we could put either of the others next. Thus a canonical form is

$$\begin{array}{c} \\ b \\ a \\ c \end{array} \begin{array}{ccc} b & a & c \\ \left(\begin{array}{ccc} 0 & 1 & 1 \\ -1 & 0 & 0 \\ -1 & 0 & 0 \end{array} \right). \end{array}$$

This demonstrates typical properties of matrices in canonical form. First of all, the diagonal entries of any order matrix are 0. Next, an object may be tied with one or more of its neighbors in the matrix; hence, in canonical form a square block of 0's will appear around the diagonals. Otherwise, an object is ahead of each of its successors in the matrix, and hence all entries above the 0's are $+1$, and all below the 0's are -1. These conditions are clearly necessary and sufficient to make a matrix an ordering matrix in canonical form. Thus the canonical form is an easy tool for determining whether a matrix is an ordering matrix. (See Exercises 2 and 3.)

Next, we must consider the relation of betweenness. Let us use the notation [A,C,B] to indicate that C is between A and B. Clearly, [A,C,B] if and only if [B,C,A]; and we also see that [A,A,B] is always true. For [A,C,B] to hold, every pairwise judgment in C must be intermediate to those in

A and B; that is, for all i and all j, either $a_{ij} \leq c_{ij} \leq b_{ij}$ or $a_{ij} \geq c_{ij} \geq b_{ij}$. We can extend this relation to more than three objects.

DEFINITION 1. *The rankings* A_1, A_2, $\cdots$, A_l *are on a line if for $i < j < k$,* $[A_i, A_j, A_k]$.

We will need one more concept:

DEFINITION 2. *A* complete ranking *is one containing no ties.*

The matrix of a complete ranking has 0's only on the diagonal; hence, in canonical form it has all $+1$'s above and -1's below the diagonal. We will have to make use of the reverse of a complete ranking. This is given by replacing a_{ij} by $-a_{ij}$, i.e., the *reverse* of the complete ranking matrix A is the matrix $-A$ which represents the ranking obtained by reversing the order of A. We shall also use the ranking O in which all objects are tied, represented by the O matrix. Clearly, for any A, $[A, O, -A]$ holds.

3. Mathematical solution of the problem. We shall now show deductively that the four axioms uniquely determine the distance d, no matter what n is, and we shall find a simple formula for distance in terms of the ordering matrices.

In general, given a set of axioms for an unknown quantity, such as d, there are three possibilities: (I) The axioms are inconsistent; i.e., there is no d satisfying all axioms. (II) There is a unique d satisfying all axioms. (III) There is more than one d. We shall show first of all that III cannot occur, by showing that the axioms leave us no freedom. This will be the major part of our proof. It then remains only to show that the axioms are consistent, by demonstrating a d satisfying all axioms; it will then follow that it is the uniquely determined distance function.

First of all we shall need a number of preliminary results, or lemmas.

LEMMA 1. *If A_1, A_2, $\ldots$, A_l ($l \geq 2$) are on a line, then*

$$d(A_1,A_l) = d(A_1,A_2) + d(A_2,A_3) + \cdots + d(A_{l-1},A_l).$$

Proof: This is obtained by repeated application of Axiom 1.3. The argument is made rigorous by mathematical induction on l. If $l = 2$, the formula is the identity $d(A_1,A_2) = d(A_1,A_2)$. Now let us assume the formula for $l = k$, and let us prove it for $l = k + 1$. We have A_1, A_2, $\cdots$, A_k, A_{k+1} on a line. By definition, this means that $[A_1,A_k,A_{k+1}]$; hence, by Axiom 1.3 we have

$$d(A_1,A_{k+1}) = d(A_1,A_k) + d(A_k,A_{k+1}).$$

But, by the inductive assumption applied to the first k rankings,

$$d(A_1,A_k) = d(A_1,A_2) + \cdots + d(A_{k-1},A_k).$$

Hence, the formula holds for $k + 1$. Then the lemma follows by induction. (For an interpretation see Exercise 5.)

Q.E.D.

LEMMA 2. *For $n = 2$ all distances are determined by the axioms.*

Proof: We are given two objects, a and b. There are three possible rankings; a ahead of b, b ahead of a, and a tied with b. The ordering matrices corresponding to these are

$$A = \begin{array}{c} \\ a \\ b \end{array}\begin{array}{cc} a & b \\ \end{array}\!\!\begin{pmatrix} 0 & 1 \\ -1 & 0 \end{pmatrix}, \quad -A = \begin{array}{c} \\ a \\ b \end{array}\begin{array}{cc} a & b \\ \end{array}\!\!\begin{pmatrix} 0 & -1 \\ 1 & 0 \end{pmatrix}, \quad O = \begin{array}{c} \\ a \\ b \end{array}\begin{array}{cc} a & b \\ \end{array}\!\!\begin{pmatrix} 0 & 0 \\ 0 & 0 \end{pmatrix}.$$

There are nine pairs we can form out of three objects; hence, nine distances have to be determined. Let us consider the axioms in order.

Axiom 1.1 asserts that

$$d(\text{A},\text{A}) = d(-\text{A},-\text{A}) = d(\text{O},\text{O}) = 0,$$

and that the other six distances are positive.

Axiom 1.2 asserts that

$$d(\text{A},-\text{A}) = d(-\text{A},\text{A}); \quad d(\text{A},\text{O}) = d(\text{O},\text{A}); \quad d(-\text{A},\text{O}) = d(\text{O},-\text{A}).$$

Hence only three distances need to be determined.

Since $[\text{A},\text{O},-\text{A}]$, Axiom 1.3 asserts that

$$d(\text{A},-\text{A}) = d(\text{A},\text{O}) + d(\text{O},-\text{A}).$$

Hence only two distances remain.

$-\text{A}$ results from A by interchanging a and b, and O is unchanged by this permutation. Hence, from Axiom 2,

$$d(-\text{A},\text{O}) = d(\text{A},\text{O}).$$

Hence, only $d(\text{A},\text{O})$ remains. But it is clear from the above that this is the minimum positive distance; hence, by Axiom 4,

$$d(\text{A},\text{O}) = 1.$$

Q.E.D.

We succeeded in determining all distances for $n = 2$. The resulting geometric configuration is a simple line-segment of total length 2, shown in Figure 1.

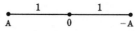

Figure 1

Notice that we did not even have to use Axiom 3. This is not surprising, since this axiom has a non-trivial content only if $n \geq 3$.

LEMMA 3. *For any n, for a complete ranking* A, $d(\text{A},-\text{A}) = n(n-1)$, *and* $d(\text{A},\text{O}) = n(n-1)/2$.

Proof: Construct the line from A to $-\text{A}$, as in Exercises 6 and 7. Then, by Lemma 1, $d(\text{A},-\text{A})$ is the sum of the $n(n-1)/2$ small distances. In each intermediate distance we have simply interchanged two neighbors; hence we have changed only a segment of length 2. Thus, by Axiom 3, these distances can be computed as if n were 2. Lemma 2 then tells us that such a distance is 2. Thus $d(\text{A},-\text{A}) = 2[n(n-1)/2] = n(n-1)$.

But $[\text{A},\text{O},-\text{A}]$; hence $d(\text{A},\text{O}) + d(-\text{A},\text{O}) = d(\text{A},-\text{A}) = n(n-1)$. And $d(\text{A},\text{O}) = d(-\text{A},\text{O})$, since one results from the other by a permutation (namely, reversing the order of objects). Hence, $d(\text{A},\text{O}) = n(n-1)/2$.

Q.E.D.

The difficulty in determining distances lies in the fact that we have convenient methods for measuring distances only along lines. Lemma 3 shows how to measure the distance from a complete ranking to its reverse (which will, of course, turn out to be a maximal possible distance), by connecting them by a line. Then O falls halfway between them. To be able to handle other rankings, we will want them between O and a complete ranking. This is accomplished by the next lemma.

LEMMA 4. *If* $\text{A}_0 \neq \text{O}$, *then there are rankings* A_1, $\ldots$, A_l *such that* A_l *is a complete ranking*, A_{i+1} *results from* A_i *by changing a segment, and* O, A_0, A_1, $\ldots$, A_l *lie on a line*.

Proof: Let us write A_0 in canonical form. Since it is not O, all blocks of 0's are smaller than $n \times n$. We form A_1 by taking the first block of 0's and putting $+1$'s above the diagonal, and -1's below the diagonal. Then A_2 is formed by doing the same to the second block, etc. If there are l blocks, then A_l will have 0's only on the diagonal; hence, it is complete.

Each A_i is in canonical form; hence, it is an ordering matrix, and the rankings are clearly on a line. Since each block represents a segment, the lemma follows.

Q.E.D.

LEMMA 5. *If it is false that* $[\text{A},\text{O},\text{B}]$, *then there are rankings* A, A_1, A_2, B *on a line, such that each is gotten from the previous one by changing a proper segment.*

Proof: If O is not between A and B, then there is an $a_{ij} = b_{ij}$ which is $+1$ or -1. We may as well assume that it is $+1$, since if it is -1 then we see that $a_{ji} = b_{ji} = +1$.

We form A_1 from A by altering that segment of A which consists of all objects which are preferred to the object i and of i itself. (This is a proper segment, since j is not included.) We simply select from this segment objects rated below i in B, and move them below i, in the original order. Next we form A_2 from A_1 by rearranging the segment after i, so that the order in this segment agrees with the ordering of these objects in B.

Hence, A_2 can differ from B only in the initial segment of B with respect to i. (This is again a proper segment.) We may thus change A_2 into B by changing only an initial segment.

Q.E.D.

The following example, with $n = 10$, illustrates the procedure of Lemma 5. We suppose that the rankings A and B are given, in which $a_{ij} = b_{ij} = +1$, and we construct A_1 and A_2.

$$A = \begin{bmatrix} a \\ b \\ c \\ i \\ d \\ e \\ f \\ j \\ g \\ h \end{bmatrix}, \quad A_1 = \begin{bmatrix} a \\ i \\ b \\ c \\ d \\ e \\ f \\ j \\ g \\ h \end{bmatrix}, \quad A_2 = \begin{bmatrix} a \\ i \\ g \\ e \\ b \\ c \\ h \\ j \\ f \\ d \end{bmatrix}, \quad B = \begin{bmatrix} g \\ a \\ i \\ e \\ b \\ c \\ h \\ j \\ f \\ d \end{bmatrix}.$$

THEOREM 1. *The axioms determine d completely for any $n \geq 2$.*

Proof: We proceed by induction on n.

If $n = 2$, then Lemma 2 shows that d is determined.

Now assume that all distances are determined for $n < k$, and consider a distance $d(A,B)$ between two rankings of k objects.

The inductive assumption becomes useful in the light of Axiom 3. This axiom now becomes the most important assumption. Suppose that A and B differ only on a segment. Then, by Axiom 3, the distance can be computed as if there were fewer than k objects, and—by the inductive assumption—all such distances are known. Thus we may assume that we know the distance between any two rankings that differ only on a segment.

CASE 1. [A,O,B]. Then $d(A,B) = d(A,O) + d(O,B)$. We will show that $d(A,O)$ is determined. If $A = O$, then $d(A,O) = 0$. If $A \neq O$, then we carry out the construction of Lemma 4. Since the rankings lie on a line, by Lemma 1

$$d(O,A_l) = d(O,A) + d(A,A_1) + \cdots + d(A_{l-1},A_l).$$

The distance on the left is $k(k-1)/2$, by Lemma 3. The last l distances on the right all involve only segments, hence they are determined, and thus $d(\text{o},\text{A}) = d(\text{A},\text{o})$ is determined. Similarly, $d(\text{o},\text{B})$ is determined, and hence also $d(\text{A},\text{B})$.

CASE 2. o is *not* between A and B. Then we carry out the construction of Lemma 5. $d(\text{A},\text{B}) = d(\text{A},\text{A}_1) + d(\text{A}_1,\text{A}_2) + d(\text{A}_2,\text{B})$ by Lemma 1. Since the three distances on the right involve only changes in segments, they are determined. Hence $d(\text{A},\text{B})$ is determined.

Thus for $n = k$ all distances are determined. Hence, the theorem follows by induction.

Q.E.D.

Let us illustrate the steps of the proof for $n = 3$. The resulting geometric configuration is a hexagon, as in Figure 2.

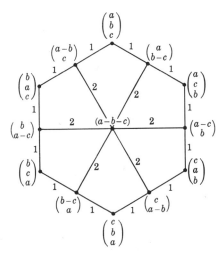

Figure 2   The rankings of three objects

If we compare rankings on one side of the hexagon, then we are changing only a segment of length 2; hence, the distances on each side are as in Figure 1. For example, on the upper right side a is always first, and only b and c are being rearranged.

Case 1 occurs when we measure a distance through the center (which is 0). The missing distance is between $\text{A} = \begin{pmatrix} a \\ b-c \end{pmatrix}$ and the center. Since A has one block of ties, $\text{A}_l = \text{A}_1$ is either $\begin{pmatrix} a \\ b \\ c \end{pmatrix}$ or $\begin{pmatrix} a \\ c \\ b \end{pmatrix}$. We know, then, that

$d(A_1,O) = n(n - 1)/2 = 3$, and that $d(A,A_1) = 1$; hence, the missing distance is 2.

Case 2 arises when the shortest distance is measured around the perimeter. For example, let $A = \begin{pmatrix} a \\ b \\ c \end{pmatrix}$, $B = \begin{pmatrix} b \\ c \\ a \end{pmatrix}$. Then $A_1 = \begin{pmatrix} b \\ a \\ c \end{pmatrix}$; a has been moved below b. Next $A_2 = \begin{pmatrix} b \\ c \\ a \end{pmatrix}$; a has been moved below c. And, by chance, $A_2 = B$; and hence, the third change is not needed. Thus, we see that $d(A,B) = 2 + 2 + 0 = 4$.

THEOREM 2. *The definition*

$$d(A,B) = \tfrac{1}{2} \sum_{i,j} |a_{ij} - b_{ij}|$$

defines the unique d that satisfies all axioms.

Proof: We know from Theorem 1 that the axioms determine d, if there is such a distance function. We need only verify that the distance defined above satisfies the axioms.

The distance is a sum of absolute values; hence, it cannot be negative. It is 0 only if every term is 0, which means that $a_{ij} = b_{ij}$ for all i and j; i.e., that $A = B$. Hence, Axiom 1.1 holds.

Axiom 1.2 follows from the fact that $|a_{ij} - b_{ij}| = |b_{ij} - a_{ij}|$.

It is easily demonstrated for absolute values that

$$|a_{ij} - b_{ij}| + |b_{ij} - c_{ij}| \geq |a_{ij} - c_{ij}|.$$

If we sum these inequalities for all i and j and divide through by 2, we obtain $d(A,B) + d(B,C) \geq d(A,C)$. The only way we can come out with an equality is to have equality for each i and j, and so that b_{ij} is between a_{ij} and c_{ij} for all i and j. But, this is precisely the condition that B be between A and C. Hence Axiom 1.3 follows.

A permutation of objects simply rearranges the rows and columns of the ordering matrix. Thus if A' results from A by a permutation, and B' from B by the same permutation, then $d(A',B')$ is the sum of the same terms as $d(A,B)$, except for the fact that the terms occur in different order. Thus Axiom 2 is verified.

Suppose that A and B differ only on a segment of length k. Write A in canonical form, and write B using the same order for the objects. (This rearrangement does not affect $d(A,B)$, as we have just verified.) In this form A and B agree except for a $k \times k$ submatrix, "in the middle," corresponding to the segment. Thus $|a_{ij} - b_{ij}|$ is 0 except possibly on the submatrix, and hence the sum is the same as if we used the two $k \times k$ submatrices to compute the distance. This establishes Axiom 3.

Using properties (I) and (II) of an ordering matrix we immediately see that d is always an integer (possibly 0). Since we can also verify that for $n = 2$, $d(\text{A},\text{O}) = 1$, as in Figure 1, 1 is indeed the minimum positive distance. This verifies Axiom 4.

Q.E.D.

4. Interpretation of the mathematical results. We can now answer the three questions asked at the end of Section 1: (1) Our axioms are consistent. (2) There is a unique distance function satisfying all axioms. (3) No additional assumptions are needed. Therefore, if we have agreed on the four axioms as reasonable assumptions, then we *must* accept the resulting definition of distance. We have thus given an example of a successful explication of an intuitive scientific concept. (See Chapter I.)

The resulting distance may be described as follows: Compare the rankings A and B for each pair of individuals i and j. If the two rankings agree, we write down 0. If one prefers i to j and the other j to i, we write down 2. And if one expresses a preference when the other indicates a tie, we write down 1. Once we have these numbers written down for all pairs i and j, $d(\text{A},\text{B})$ equals the sum of these numbers.

Had we written down this definition to start with, we might have thought it a fairly reasonable way to measure the distance between two rankings. However, had other equally reasonable-sounding definitions been suggested, we would have had no rational way of choosing among them. With our present procedure the argument is limited to one concerned with satisfying the four axioms stated above. Anyone who accepts those four conditions *must* accept the resulting definition of d. Hence, anyone who rejects our definition of a distance must specify which of our conditions he rejects, and should be forced to give conditions of his own which are reasonable and which lead to a unique choice of the distance function. In this way an argument about a sociological problem can be put on a useful plane.

Let us now apply the distance function to the construction of consensus rankings. Although our discussion will be quite general, we shall refer for concreteness to the ranking of three objects as in Figure 2.

If a number of experts rank our n objects, each ranking will be a point in the geometrical space. For example, if $n = 3$, each expert selects one of the 13 points in Figure 2. The consensus ranking should be the point that is in best agreement with the set of selected rankings. Two reasonable selections of this point are given as follows:

DEFINITION 3. *If* $\text{A}_1, \ldots, \text{A}_m$ *are a set of points (not necessarily distinct), the* median *of the set is that point* B *(or those points) for which* $\sum_{i=1}^{m} d(\text{A}_i,\text{B})$ *is a minimum. The* mean *is that point* B *(or those points) for which* $\sum_{i=1}^{m} d(\text{A}_i,\text{B})^2$ *is a minimum.*

A justification for such a method of consensus ranking may be given as follows. Let us suppose that the ranking we wish is the consensus ranking of the entire population. But we cannot afford such a poll, so we select some "experts" at random. It follows † from a more general theorem that if the sample chosen is sufficiently large, then the probability that the consensus arrived at is the desired one is very nearly 1. And we may make this probability as near to certainty as desired by increasing the sample.

Unfortunately, this justification works for many different methods of arriving at a consensus. For example, it applies both to medians and to means.

Let us consider two examples. Suppose that three experts are asked to rank three objects, and that two arrive at $\begin{pmatrix} a \\ b \\ c \end{pmatrix}$, while the third one decides on $\begin{pmatrix} b \\ a \\ c \end{pmatrix}$. From Figure 2, we can see that the median is $\begin{pmatrix} a \\ b \\ c \end{pmatrix}$, since for this point the sum of the distances to the three given rankings is $0 + 0 + 2 = 2$, while from any other point it is at least 3. On the other hand, the mean is $\begin{pmatrix} a-b \\ c \end{pmatrix}$, for which the sum of the squares of the distances is 3, a minimum.

Thus, each method ranks c last, as did each of the experts. The dispute concerns the ranking of a versus b, since two experts put a ahead, and one puts b ahead. The median in this case yields the majority verdict, whereas the mean decides that the evidence is inconclusive and reports a tie. Both results seem reasonable.

Next we will consider the worst possible outcome, where there is "complete disagreement" among the experts: They report respectively

$$\begin{pmatrix} a \\ b \\ c \end{pmatrix}, \quad \begin{pmatrix} b \\ c \\ a \end{pmatrix}, \quad \text{and} \quad \begin{pmatrix} c \\ a \\ b \end{pmatrix}.$$

The mean in this case is the center point, a three-way tie. We find that, instead of a unique median, there are three points (namely, the three rankings of the experts), each of which yields the minimum value of 8. Hence, the median tells you to "take your pick among the experts," while the mean decides to tie the objects. Again, each method may appear reasonable, although the results are quite different.

The definitions of mean and median given above are generalizations of the classical definition which we have if we apply Definition 3 to a set of points on a line. The principal difference is that in our application these consensus rankings need not be unique. But even in the classical case

† See John G. Kemeny, "Generalized random variables," *Pacific Journal of Mathematics*, Vol. 9 (1959), pp. 1179–1189.

medians need not be unique, although means always happen to be so. These concepts enable one to carry out a certain amount of statistical work on rankings of experts, and hence are a useful tool for the social scientist.

EXERCISES

1. Prove that properties (1) through (8) for ordering matrices given in Section 2 are equivalent to properties (I) through (III).

2. Prove that, if A is an ordering matrix, then arranging its rows according to the number of $+1$ entries (largest number coming first) will put it into canonical form.

3. Prove that a matrix that is not an ordering matrix cannot be put into canonical form. Devise a simple test for determining whether a given matrix is an ordering matrix.

4. Show that, if in plane geometry we interpret [A,C,B] as saying that the point C lies on the line-segment connecting points A and B, then Definition 1 agrees with the geometric concept of points lying on a line in the specified order.

5. Show that Lemma 1 holds for plane geometry. Show that the restriction that the points lie on a line is really necessary.

6. Show that a complete ranking A can be changed into its reverse ranking $-A$ through a series of rankings $A = A_0, A_1, A_2, \ldots, A_l = -A$; where A_{i+1} results from A_i by interchanging two objects that are next to each other in the ranking A_i. Show that this can be done so that the rankings lie on a line.

7. In Exercise 6 show that $l = n(n-1)/2$.

8. Give an intuitive interpretation for the procedure of Lemma 4.

9. Prove that, if $A \neq B$, the $d(A,B)$ is a positive integer.

10. Illustrate all possible distances for rankings of four objects.

11. Sketch the geometry of the rankings of four objects. (*Hint:* o can be chosen as the center of a semi-regular solid, i.e. a solid bounded by two kinds of regular polygons. The other points lie on the surface.)

12. Find the median(s) and mean(s) for each of the following sets of 3 rankings:

(1) $\qquad A = \begin{pmatrix} a \\ b \\ c \end{pmatrix}, \quad B = \begin{pmatrix} c \\ a \\ b \end{pmatrix}, \quad C = \begin{pmatrix} a \\ c \\ b \end{pmatrix}.$

(2) $\qquad A = \begin{pmatrix} a \\ b \\ c \end{pmatrix}, \quad B = \begin{pmatrix} a \\ b{-}c \end{pmatrix}, \quad C = \begin{pmatrix} b{-}c \\ a \end{pmatrix}.$

(3) $\qquad A = \begin{pmatrix} a{-}b \\ c \end{pmatrix}, \quad B = \begin{pmatrix} a{-}c \\ b \end{pmatrix}, \quad C = \begin{pmatrix} b{-}c \\ a \end{pmatrix}.$

13. Find the median(s) and mean(s) for each of the following sets of 5 rankings:

(1)
$$A = \begin{pmatrix} a \\ b \\ c \end{pmatrix}, \quad B = \begin{pmatrix} a{-}b \\ c \end{pmatrix}, \quad C = \begin{pmatrix} a{-}c \\ b \end{pmatrix},$$

$$D = \begin{pmatrix} b{-}c \\ a \end{pmatrix}, \quad E = \begin{pmatrix} c \\ a{-}b \end{pmatrix}.$$

(2)
$$A = B = \begin{pmatrix} a \\ b \\ c \end{pmatrix}, \quad C = \begin{pmatrix} b \\ a{-}c \end{pmatrix}, \quad D = E = \begin{pmatrix} c \\ b \\ a \end{pmatrix}.$$

(3)
$$A = B = C = D = \begin{pmatrix} a \\ b \\ c \end{pmatrix}, \quad E = \begin{pmatrix} c \\ b \\ a \end{pmatrix}.$$

14. Suggest a measure of the reliability of the consensus ranking. (*Hint:* it should be very good if all the experts agree, and very poor if the judgments are widely scattered.)

15. Prove that, if three experts submit rankings such that [A,B,C], then B is the unique median. Extend this result to five experts. What can you say about four experts in such a case?

16. Show by an example that the results of Exercise 15 do not hold for means.

17. Propose criteria that would lead one to prefer means to medians, or medians to means.

PROJECT 1

Develop a measure of the reliability of a consensus ranking by k experts. For example, this may be based on the largest possible change that can be brought about by changing the ranking of a single expert. (Attention must be paid to the possibility of multiple consensus rankings.)

Prove some theorems concerning the most and least reliable consensuses possible for a given k.

PROJECT 2

It is desired to organize a group of people into committees. The following conditions are agreed upon:

1. Each committee must have exactly three members.
2. Each person must serve on exactly two committees.
3. For any given committee there must be exactly two other committees with non-overlapping membership (i.e., having no member in common with the given committee).

The first two conditions are self-explanatory; the last is motivated by a desire to hold simultaneous committee meetings. Prove theorems concerning the possible number of men in the entire group, and concerning the number of committees. Show that although the possibilities for organizing such a group are limited, there is more than one way of meeting all three conditions. Propose an additional requirement that will narrow the possibilities to a single solution. (This condition should *not* be in terms of the number of people or number of committees desired.)

CHAPTER III

Ecology

Two Dynamic Models

1. The problem. We shall consider the interdependence of two species, the first of which serves as food for the second one. The discussion will be based on a more general model in Lotka, Chapter VIII. To make the discussion more concrete, we shall think of the first species as consisting of rabbits, the second of foxes. But models of this general type have much wider applicability. To mention but one example that is quite different from rabbits and foxes, consider the spread of a fatal disease by means of bacteria. We can then take the human population of the region as the first species, and the bacteria as the second one.

Let us consider the first species in isolation. If there are no foxes to kill the rabbits, then the rabbit population will expand. (We shall assume throughout this chapter that other factors influencing the growth of the two species remain constant; only the numbers in the two species are treated as variable.) The simplest assumption that can be made, and one that is quite realistic, is that the rate of increase of the rabbit population is proportional to the size of the population. Letting x be the number of rabbits and y the number of foxes at time t, we obtain:

$$(1) \qquad \text{If} \quad y = 0, \quad \text{then} \quad \frac{dx}{dt} = ax, \quad a > 0.$$

On the other hand, if there are no rabbits to feed on, the foxes slowly die out, so that we have the following:

$$(2) \qquad \text{If} \quad x = 0. \quad \text{then} \quad \frac{dy}{dt} = -py, \quad p > 0.$$

On the other hand, if there are both rabbits and foxes, we must take the interaction of the species into account. We shall assume that the number of kills of rabbits by foxes is proportional to xy. We then modify (2) by adding a term proportional to xy to allow for the increase of foxes in the presence of food, and we subtract such a term from (1) to take into account the unnatural deaths of rabbits due to foxes.

(3) $\dfrac{dx}{dt} = ax - bxy;$ $\dfrac{dy}{dt} = cxy - py;$ $a, b, c, p > 0.$

We have thus arrived at a dynamic model for the interaction of the two species. We make a count of the number in each at a given time, which we may as well call $t = 0$, and find $x = x_0 > 0$ rabbits and $y = y_0 > 0$ foxes. Our main task will be to determine what the model predicts about the sizes of the two populations for the future.

It will be interesting to consider a second model, similar in form, but leading to quite different solutions. Suppose that we consider two species of hunters that are in competition with each other, so that members of one species often kill members of the other species. Each one has a natural rate of increase in the absence of its enemy, with expansion rates with parameters a,p. Each species decreases proportionally to the product xy as a result of kills by the other species. Hence, the simplest model is given by

(3′) $\dfrac{dx}{dt} = ax - bxy;$ $\dfrac{dy}{dt} = py - cxy;$ $a, b, c, p > 0.$

We will again start with given sizes for the two species and try to find out what the model predicts for the future.

2. The differential equations. The equations of the model are examples of a particularly interesting type of simultaneous first order differential equations. They are of the form:

(4) $\dfrac{dx}{dt} = F(x,y);$ $\dfrac{dy}{dt} = G(x,y).$

These equations have the special property that time does not enter them explicitly. As a matter of fact, time can be eliminated by dividing the second equation by the first:

(5) $\dfrac{dy}{dx} = G(x,y)/F(x,y).$

Often, we are interested only in the possible values of the quantities x and y, which we shall represent geometrically by the position of the points (x,y). As we do not care to know the exact times when these positions are occupied, (5) furnishes all interesting information. The locus of the position through time, known as the *trajectory*, must be a solution of the first order differential equation (5).

Such equations have been studied extensively (see Lefschetz, Chapters II and V). We shall summarize only a few of the known results. The most important one is the following existence and uniqueness theorem.

THEOREM 1. *If (x_0,y_0) is a point of the plane near which the partial derivatives of F and G are continuous, then there is a unique solution of (4) passing through (x_0,y_0), at $t = 0$. The solutions are either constant functions of time, or they describe a simple curve. Furthermore, the solutions $x(t)$ and $y(t)$ depend continuously on the initial position.*

We will not attempt to give a proof of this theorem. However, we can draw many useful conclusions from it.

First of all, we note that in our case the trajectories do not depend on the starting time. Thus if $x(t_0) = x_0$, $y(t_0) = y_0$ at a certain time t_0, then for any time after t_0 the trajectories are as if the process at time 0 started at (x_0,y_0); that is, $x(t - t_0)$ and $y(t - t_0)$ agree with the functions $x'(t)$ and $y'(t)$ which one would have if $x(0) = x_0$ and $y(0) = y_0$. Hence, there is a unique trajectory through each point. An immediate consequence is that two trajectories cannot cross, for we would then have two different trajectories through the same point. A trajectory also cannot cross itself, since by (4) the direction of motion depends only on the position, not on the time. The trajectories given by Theorem 1 are, of course, solutions of (5).

We must now discuss solutions that are constant functions of time. These occur at *equilibrium points;* that is, points where $F = G = 0$. If we choose such a point as the starting position, then the rates of change in (4) are 0, and so we remain at the starting point. We thus have a one-point trajectory.

If the starting point is not an equilibrium point, then the trajectory is a simple curve. Furthermore, this curve must be traversed in a fixed direction, since (4) determines the direction of motion for every point of the trajectory. This direction could be reversed only if we reached an equilibrium point, or if the curve crossed itself, which is impossible. However, an equilibrium point cannot lie on a curve trajectory: If it did, the curve trajectory would have a point in common with the point trajectory, and we would have two trajectories through the same point. Thus, an equilibrium point can never be reached if we start out of equilibrium. But this does not prevent the trajectory from approaching the equilibrium point asymptotically. That is, the position gets closer and closer to the equilibrium position, although it never reaches it in finite time. The equilibrium is the limit of the position as $t \to \infty$.

It is of particular interest to note how a trajectory behaves in the neighborhood of an equilibrium point. We shall illustrate three kinds of behavior in this chapter and the next one: (1) Whenever we start near the equilibrium, we approach the equilibrium. This is known as a *stable* equilibrium point. (2) Whenever we start near the equilibrium, we proceed away from it; such an equilibrium is known as *unstable*. (3) Whenever the trajectory is a closed curve with the equilibrium point on the inside, we move cyclically around the equilibrium.

A major tool in determining the nature of the behavior is given in the following theorem, whereas a more thorough discussion is presented in Appendix F.

THEOREM 2. *The nature of a trajectory near an equilibrium point may be determined by expanding F and G in a Taylor series around the equilibrium, and keeping only linear terms. The solutions of these linear equations near the equilibrium will have the same general nature as the exact solutions.*

In this chapter we consider only two equations in two unknowns. But the discussion just concluded holds equally well (with the obvious modifications) when there are n equations in n unknowns:

$$(6) \qquad \frac{dx_i}{dt} = F_i(x_1, \ldots, x_n) \quad \text{for } i = 1, \ldots, n.$$

Examples will be found in the next chapter.

3. Solution of the equations. At first we will concentrate on the model generated by the equations in (3). We shall be interested only in trajectories in the first quadrant. Our first task will be to show that if $x_0 > 0$ and $y_0 > 0$, then $x(t) > 0$ and $y(t) > 0$ for all t.

Let us start by discussing four special trajectories. First, there are only two equilibrium points, $(0,0)$ and $E = (p/c, a/b)$. Thus we have two one-point trajectories. But the positive parts of the axes are also trajectories. (For the behavior on these axes and near the origin see Exercises 1 to 3.) Since trajectories cannot cross, a trajectory starting inside the first quadrant can never cross either axis, and hence $x(t) > 0$ and $y(t) > 0$ for all time.

The interesting equilibrium point is E. Let us find the nature of the trajectories near E. Let $u = x - p/c$ and $v = y - a/b$. Then $du/dt = dx/dt = -(u + p/c)bv$; and $dv/dt = dy/dt = cu(v + a/b)$. The linear parts of these equations are

$$(7) \qquad \frac{du}{dt} \approx -\frac{bp}{c}v; \quad \frac{dv}{dt} \approx \frac{ac}{b}u.$$

Treating these as exact equations in accord with Theorem 2, differentiating the first equation, and substituting dv/dt from the second, we obtain

$$(8) \qquad d^2u/dt^2 = -apu.$$

The motion will therefore be periodic. Since the starting time is unimportant, let us start at a time when $u = 0$. The solution of (8) is then $u = A \sin (\sqrt{ap}\, t)$; and from (7) we obtain a solution of the form $v = B \cos (\sqrt{ap}\, t)$. Thus $u^2/A^2 + v^2/B^2 = 1$; hence, the trajectory is an ellipse.

We have thus shown that near E the trajectories are periodic movements around the equilibrium point. In first approximation the trajectories are elliptical, and the period of revolution is $2\pi/\sqrt{ap}$.

To find the trajectories exactly, we form the equation corresponding to (5).

(9)
$$\frac{dy}{dx} = \frac{y(cx - p)}{x(a - by)}.$$

Hence

$$\frac{a - by}{y} \cdot \frac{dy}{dx} + \frac{p - cx}{x} = 0.$$

Integrating with respect to x, we obtain

$$a \log y - by + p \log x - cx = \log k$$

or

(10)
$$\frac{x^p}{e^{cx}} \cdot \frac{y^a}{e^{by}} = k.$$

Since k does not depend on time,

$$k = \frac{x_0^{\,p}}{e^{cx_0}} \cdot \frac{y_0^{\,a}}{e^{by_0}}.$$

We have thus found an equation for the trajectory corresponding to a given starting position. The function x^p/e^{cx}, or the like function y^a/e^{by} has a graph similar to Figure 3 (see Exercise 5), and so each possible value is taken on twice, except for the extreme values.

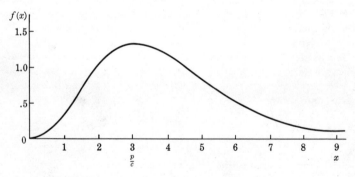

Figure 3 $f(x) = \dfrac{x^p}{e^{cx}}$ for $c = 1$, $p = 3$

Thus if in (10) we fix x at a possible value, there are normally two corresponding y-values, and for a possible y-value there are normally two possible x-values. Thus we obtain a simple closed curve. The maximum and minimum y-values are taken on for $x = p/c$, while the maximum and minimum x-values occur for $y = a/b$, and there are no inflection points. (See Exercise 6.) A family of such trajectories is shown in Figure 4.

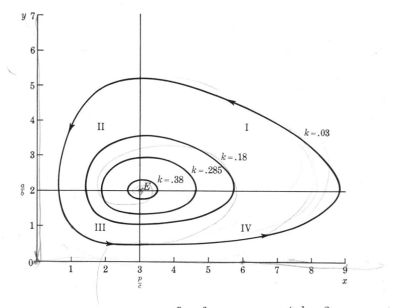

Figure 4 Trajectories $\dfrac{x^p}{e^{cx}} \cdot \dfrac{y^a}{e^{by}} = k$ for $\begin{array}{l} a = 4,\ b = 2 \\ c = 1,\ p = 3 \end{array}$

We must still determine the direction of motion. From (3), $dx/dt > 0$ if and only if $y < a/b$. Hence, on the lower half of the trajectory x is increasing, whereas on the upper it is decreasing. Therefore, motion must be counterclockwise.

As a final result we shall obtain the average values $\bar{x}$ and $\bar{y}$. Since the motion is cyclic, we may take the average over one cycle. Let T be the length of a cycle. From (3),

$$\frac{1}{x}\frac{dx}{dt} = a - by,$$

$$\int_0^T \frac{1}{x}\frac{dx}{dt}\, dt = \int_0^T (a - by)\, dt,$$

(11) $\log{(x(T))} - \log{(x(0))} = aT - b\displaystyle\int_0^T y\, dt = T[a - b\bar{y}].$

But $(0,T)$ is a complete cycle; hence $x(0) = x(T)$. Thus the left side of (11) is 0, and hence so is the right side. Thus $\bar{y} = a/b$. And similarly, $\bar{x} = p/c$. These averages turn out to be independent of the initial position and hence are the same as the equilibrium values at E.

Let us now turn to the second model, which is generated by the equations in $(3')$. We find the same equilibrium points as before, and the axes are again special trajectories. Thus a trajectory starting with positive values for x and y will continue to have positive values. The major difference arises when we find the behavior near E. By the approximation used in (7) we find

$$(7') \qquad du/dt = -(bp/c)v; \quad dv/dt = -(ac/b)u.$$

And thus,

$$(8') \qquad d^2u/dt^2 = apu.$$

In this case the solution is *not* periodic. The most general solution of this equation is $u = Ae^{st} + Be^{-st}$, where $s = \sqrt{ap}$. If we differentiate this and substitute the result in $(7')$, we obtain $v = -rAe^{st} + rBe^{-st}$, in which $r = cs/bp$. From these solutions we find the relation $u^2 - (v/r)^2 = 4AB$; hence, the first approximation trajectories are hyperbolas, with E as center.

Therefore, we know that the motion is not periodic, and that the trajectories approach the equilibrium point for a while—and then run away from it. To obtain more information concerning the trajectories we carry out the method of Equations (9) and (10) to find:

$$(9') \qquad \frac{dy}{dx} = \frac{y(p - cx)}{x(a - by)},$$

and

$$(10') \qquad \frac{y^a}{e^{by}} = k\,\frac{x^p}{e^{cx}} \; ; \quad k = \frac{y_0{}^a e^{cx_0}}{e^{by_0}x_0{}^p}.$$

Particularly interesting are the curves passing through E, i.e., where

$$k = \frac{\left(\dfrac{a}{b}\right)^a e^{c(p/c)}}{e^{b(a/b)}\left(\dfrac{p}{c}\right)^p} = \left(\frac{a}{b}\right)^a \left(\frac{c}{p}\right)^p e^{p-a}.$$

These are shown by heavy lines in Figure 5. Since trajectories cannot cross, and since E is a point trajectory, the remainder of these curves must actually represent four separate trajectories. By considering the signs of the derivatives in $(7')$, we see that two of these correspond to asymptotic approach to the equilibrium E whereas two represent asymptotic regress from the equilibrium.

These curves divide the positive quadrant into four regions. If the process starts in a given region it must stay there. The shape of a trajectory and the direction of motion is then determined by the signs of dy/dx and d^2y/dx^2. Representative examples are shown in Figure 5.

There is, of course, no analogue to (11), since the motion is not periodic.

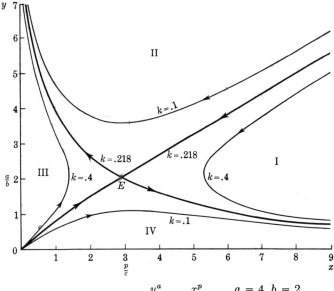

Figure 5   Trajectories $\dfrac{y^a}{e^{by}} = k\,\dfrac{x^p}{e^{cx}}$ for $\begin{aligned} a &= 4,\, b = 2 \\ c &= 1,\, p = 3 \end{aligned}$

4. Interpretation of the results. In the model for (3) we have cyclic behavior. Our cycle always starts with a positive number of rabbits and foxes. It is extremely unlikely that we should start exactly with the equilibrium values; hence, we may assume that we shall follow a closed curve trajectory, as in Figure 4. We shall therefore observe a cyclic process of four stages: (I) Rabbits are in abundance. The number of foxes increases, cutting down on the number of rabbits. (II) When the rabbits drop to $x = p/c$, the foxes find insufficient food and hence start declining in number. Rabbits continue to decline. (III) When foxes drop to $y = a/b$ in number, rabbits can start increasing in number. Foxes continue to decline. (IV) When rabbits get back up to $x = p/c$, foxes start increasing again, until they reach a level of $y = a/b$. At this point Stage I is reentered. The fact that the trajectories can never reach an axis means that neither species will ever be wiped out. Thus, we have a type of cyclic equilibrium.

The average number of rabbits is p/c, and of foxes a/b, independently of the starting stocks. Thus, the equilibrium values are determined by the machinery of change, given by (3), and not by the starting values. The starting values influence only how widely the values vary. The further we start from equilibrium, the wider the variation.

Figure 4 shows four closed trajectories for the case $a = 4$, $b = 2$, $c = 1$, $p = 3$. The equilibrium point is $E = (3,2)$. The curves, from the inside out, correspond to starting positions $(3, 1.75)$; $(3, 1.3)$; $(3,1)$; and $(3, .5)$. The trajectories were traced out by numerical approximation on a computing machine.

It is seen that the innermost trajectory is very nearly an ellipse, whereas the ones further out become more "lopsided." Our first approximation solution for the length of the cycle yields $T = 2\pi/\sqrt{ap} = 1.814$. The numerical estimates of the trajectories yield (to two decimal places) 1.81, 1.84, 1.88, and 2.04, respectively. Thus the approximation is excellent near E, and it is fairly good even further out. Thus, although the sizes of the species vary greatly according to the initial stocks, the times of revolution change very little for reasonable values.

In the model for (3′) we note that the normal asymptotic behavior is one of approaching an axis. That is, although no species dies out in finite time, one tends to vanish asymptotically. If we take into account that there cannot be less than one animal per species, this really amounts to the prediction of the eventual extinction of one species. The other species, on the other hand, tends to infinity. Of course this too is an oversimplification, in that the model neglects shortages of the food supply.

There are again four important regions, but this time they determine the long-range outcome: (I) There are large numbers of both species to start with. This causes a steady decrease in both species (because of the large number of kills), until the second species drops to the critical level of $y = a/b$. Then the first species starts to increase again and is able to wipe its enemy out. (II) This is like I, except that the critical level is $x = p/c$, and it is the first species that is eliminated. (III) There are small numbers to start with, and hence very little conflict. Thus each species can increase, until the second species reaches the critical level of $y = a/b$. Then it begins to dominate the first species, and eventually eliminates it. (IV) This is like III, except for the fact that the critical level is $x = p/c$, and it is the second species that dies out.

The exceptions to these rules occur on the boundaries of the regions, which consist of the four special trajectories marked heavily in Figure 5, and of the point E itself. The boundary of I and IV shares with both regions the feature that the second species is wiped out, but the increase in the first species and the decrease in the second both take place monotonically. The boundary of II and III is similar, with the first species being wiped out. But if the initial numbers of the two species happen to fall on the border of I and II, or of III and IV, then the numbers tend to the equilibrium values E monotonically. At E itself no change can take place. Of course, any such starting combination is very unlikely.

EXERCISES

1. Prove that $y = 0$, $x = e^{at}$ is a solution of (3) and (3′). What is the trajectory? In what direction does the process move?
2. Find solutions, like that of Exercise 1, in which $x = 0$ for each model.
3. Prove that the Taylor series expansion of (3) around (0,0) has Equations (1) and (2) as its linear part. What about (3′)? (See Appendix F.)
4. Find the trajectories corresponding to Equations (1) and (2). Describe the nature of the motion, and interpret it. Do the same for the second model.
5. Find the maximum, minimum and inflection points of the curve of x^p/e^{cx}, and verify that it must have the general shape of Figure 3. How do the cases $p > c$ and $p < c$ differ?
6. From (9), find d^2y/dx^2. Show that there are no points of inflection on the trajectory. When is the curve concave upwards? Show that the curves of (9′) do have inflection points.
7. How do the trajectories change if in (4) we replace F by $-F$ and G by $-G$?

The two models discussed are special cases of the more general model $\dfrac{dx}{dt} = x \cdot G(y)$, $\dfrac{dy}{dt} = H(x) \cdot y$, where $G(0) \neq 0$ and $H(0) \neq 0$. Exercises 8 through 13 refer to this class of models.

8. Find the equilibrium points, and describe certain special trajectories.
9. Prove that if $x_0 > 0$ and $y_0 > 0$, then $x(t) > 0$ and $y(t) > 0$ for all t.
10. Find the analogue of Equations (10) and (10′) for trajectories.
11. Prove that if the solution is periodic, of period T, then

$$\int_0^T G(y)\, dt = \int_0^T H(x)\, dt = 0.$$

12. Let (x_0, y_0) be an equilibrium point in the first quadrant other than the origin. Prove that the approximate trajectories near this point are elliptic if $G'(y_0)H'(x_0) < 0$ and hyperbolic if $G'(y_0)H'(x_0) > 0$.
13. Show that the behavior of the solutions on the axes and near the origin depends only on $G(0)$ and $H(0)$.

PROJECT

Rapoport (in Chapter IV of *Fights, Games, and Debates*) sets up a model for production and exchange between two isolated men. One produces an amount x and the other an amount y of a different good. They agree to trade a fraction q, $0 < q < 1$, of their own produce for the same fraction of the other person's product. Hence each ends up with a fraction $p = 1 - q$ of his own produce and a fraction q of the other product. Rapoport presents arguments why it is reasonable to assume that the following equations might govern such a simple two-person economic system:

$$\frac{dx}{dt} = \frac{p}{px + qy + 1} - \frac{p}{2},$$

$$\frac{dy}{dt} = \frac{p}{qx + py + 1} - \frac{p}{2}.$$

Develop this model along the lines indicated in the present chapter. Show that the production either approaches an equilibrium or one of the two men drops out of the market. Find conditions for these two cases. In the second case show that the question of which man drops out depends only on the original amounts produced by the two men.

Hint: See the second example in Appendix F.

REFERENCES

Lefschetz, Solomon. *Lectures on differential equations.* ("Annals of Mathematics Studies," No. 14.) Princeton, N. J.: Princeton University Press, 1948.

Lotka, Alfred J. *Elements of Mathematical Biology.* New York: Dover Publications, 1956.

Rapoport, Anatol. *Fights, Games, and Debates.* Ann Arbor, Mich.: University of Michigan Press, 1960.

CHAPTER IV

Market Stability
A Dynamic Model

1. Statement of the problem. We are going to consider a model for bargaining in a market place. A group of people come to the market with the intent of trading goods. They agree on the following procedure: They will choose an initial value or price for each type of good. In terms of these initial prices, each man will compute the total value of his present holdings. He will then decide, among all combinations of goods having this same value, which combination he would most like to have. He will submit this ideal demand to a "Secretary of the Market."† The Secretary will then compute the total demand on the market. If this happens to equal the total supply, the sum of the holdings of all the men in the market, he will indicate how the goods should be redistributed to make everyone happy.

It is of course unlikely that this condition of equality will occur. If it does not, it is agreed that the prices of goods that are in short supply should increase, and the prices of goods for which the demand is smaller than the supply should decrease. Taking this into account, the Secretary determines and announces new prices. The individuals then recompute the total value of their holdings. In terms of this new total value they decide again on the ideal holdings among all combinations of goods which they can afford according to the new prices. They submit these demands to the Secretary, and he again compares the total demand with the total supply. This process continues until, hopefully, a set of prices is attained for which the demand in the market equals the supply. Such a set of prices will be called an *equilibrium set*. Then each person's demands can be fulfilled.

When such a set of prices is arrived at, the individuals in the market trade until each man has his ideal holdings, and then they leave the market. It is to be emphasized that it is only when equilibrium prices are attained that any trading takes place. The model is a dynamic model for arriving at a satisfactory price structure for the goods, *not* for the trading of goods.

We shall wish to make the procedure indicated above mathematically precise, and then we shall try to answer the following questions: Will there always be at least one set of equilibrium prices? If so, will there be more than one such set? If the market starts with an arbitrary set of prices, will

† This device was suggested by H. Uzawa.

the method of successively changing the prices, indicated above, always lead to equilibrium prices? If there is more than one set of equilibrium prices, how will the final price arrived at depend on the initial prices?

2. Mathematical formulation. We must introduce a machinery for the change of prices and for the way individuals make their demands. To avoid the fiction of a "Secretary of the Market," we shall think of the prices as undergoing an actual change as a function of time. Instead of the step-by-step procedure, we shall treat the process of change as a continuous one, in which at moment t there is a given set of prices $\mathbf{p}(t)$, as a result of which individual k has a demand-of-the-moment $\mathbf{x}^{(k)}$, and these demands collectively result in a modification of the price structure. A given process of change will be successful if the prices approach an equilibrium as $t \to \infty$.

There are m individuals who do the trading, and n different commodities are traded. We shall make various assumptions about the way the prices of the goods change, and we shall be interested in their long-range behavior. We are particularly interested in conditions under which the market is *stable* in the sense that the prices always tend to equilibrium values. Our treatment is based on the work of K. Arrow and L. Hurwicz.

Vectors $\mathbf{x}$, $\mathbf{y}$, $\mathbf{z}$, $\mathbf{p}$, with n components, will be used to denote various quantities describing the market. In each case the ith component of the vector will refer to commodity number i. The letters $\mathbf{x}$, $\mathbf{y}$, $\mathbf{z}$ are reserved for *commodity bundles*, that is, the ith component will represent a quantity of the ith commodity. On the other hand, the components of $\mathbf{p}$ are the prices of the commodities. We shall use the abbreviation

$$\mathbf{p} \cdot \mathbf{x} = \sum_i p_i x_i.$$

As the market opens, each individual is the owner of a commodity bundle—say individual k owns $\mathbf{y}^{(k)}$—and these quantities remain unchanged throughout. A set of prices $\mathbf{p}$ is announced, and individual k decides that he would like to trade his bundle for a bundle $\mathbf{x}^{(k)}$.

The first requirement is that he must ask for goods of total value equal to the value of his own commodity bundle, i.e.,

$$\sum_{i=1}^{n} p_i x_i^{(k)} = \sum_{i=1}^{n} p_i y_i^{(k)}.$$

This assumption can be written more conveniently as

(1) $$\mathbf{p} \cdot \mathbf{x}^{(k)} = \mathbf{p} \cdot \mathbf{y}^{(k)}.$$

Secondly, it is assumed that each individual will choose the bundle $\mathbf{x}^{(k)}$ that "looks best to him" from among the ones he can afford. For this we assume that he has a utility function $u^{(k)}$ (see Appendix B), and

(2) $u^{(k)}(\mathbf{x}^{(k)})$ is the unique maximum, subject to (1), and to $\mathbf{x}^{(k)} \geq 0$.

We must now introduce a machinery for the change of prices. For this we define the *excess demand vector*,

$$\mathbf{z} = \sum_{k=1}^{m} \mathbf{x}^{(k)} - \sum_{k=1}^{m} \mathbf{y}^{(k)}.$$

If z_i is positive, then the total demand for good i exceeds the supply; if it is negative, then the supply exceeds the demand. The simplest possible assumption is that the rate of change of the prices is proportional to the excess demand; hence, that a small excess demand will result in a small increase in the price of the commodity, a large excess demand in a large increase, a small excess supply in a small drop in prices, etc. The model assumes further that the rate of change actually is equal to the excess demand. Thus, prices change according to the following law:

$$(3) \qquad \frac{dp_i}{dt} = z_i(\mathbf{p}), \quad i = 1, 2, \ldots, n.$$

In this we wrote $z_i(\mathbf{p})$ to emphasize that $\mathbf{z}$ depends on the choices $\mathbf{x}^{(k)}$, which in turn depend on the current prices. These first order simultaneous equations may be rewritten as the single vector equation

$$(3') \qquad \frac{d\mathbf{p}}{dt} = \mathbf{z}(\mathbf{p}).$$

These are of the form studied in Chapter III, and we shall make use of some general properties of solutions of such equations, which were discussed in the previous chapter.

It is reasonable to impose certain restrictions on $\mathbf{z}$:

(4) $\mathbf{z}$ is a continuous function of $\mathbf{p}$.

(5) $\mathbf{z}(c\mathbf{p}) = \mathbf{z}(\mathbf{p})$.

(6)   If $p_i = 0$,   then $z_i > 0$.

The first one is in effect an assumption that utility functions operate smoothly. The second states that the demands depend only on the ratios of prices, not on their absolute numerical values. If, for example, all prices doubled, then our stock would be worth twice as much on paper, but everything we wanted to buy would also cost twice as much; hence, our demands would not change. The third assumption assures us that we can always make each good desirable if we are willing to give it away free.

It should be noted that assumption (4) is often weakened by allowing $z_i(\mathbf{p})$ to tend to $+\infty$ as p_i tends to 0. All our results will still hold in this case, but the proofs would be more complicated. We will therefore use (4) in its present form for the theoretical discussion, though we will violate it in examples.

We must determine, under assumptions (1) through (6), how prices change with time. Of particular interest are the following two concepts:

DEFINITION 1. *A set of prices* **p** *is said to be an* equilibrium point *if $dp_i/dt = 0$ for all i. The economic interpretation of equilibrium is that everyone's demands can be met and there will be no goods left over. Clearly, a necessary and sufficient condition for equilibrium, by* (3) *is that*

$$\mathbf{z}(\mathbf{p}) = 0.$$

DEFINITION 2. *A market is said to be* stable *if for any initial prices* **p** > 0, **p**(t) *approaches an equilibrium point.*

3. Mathematical treatment. From Chapter III we know that the knowledge of **p** at any one moment determines its trajectory for all future time. Our study will be restricted to the study of properties of these trajectories.

THEOREM 1. *If* $\mathbf{p}(0) > 0$, *then* $\mathbf{p}(t) > 0$ *for all* $t > 0$.

This is an immediate consequence of (3), (4), and (6), because, if for some time t, $\mathbf{p}(t) = \mathbf{p}'$ with $p_i' = 0$, then the trajectory must have passed through a region around $\mathbf{p}'$ in which $z_i \neq 0$. But in this region p_i increases, and hence $\mathbf{p}'$ can not be reached.

THEOREM 2. (*Walras' law.*) $\mathbf{p} \cdot \mathbf{z} = 0$.

Proof: From (1), $\mathbf{p} \cdot [\mathbf{x}^{(k)} - \mathbf{y}^{(k)}] = 0$, for each individual k.

If we sum these equations on k, then the theorem follows by the definition of **z**.
                                                                    Q.E.D.

THEOREM 3. *The trajectory lies on the surface of an n-dimensional sphere.*

Proof: From Theorem 2, and (3), $\sum\limits_{i=1}^{n} p_i \dfrac{dp_i}{dt} = 0$.

Integrating with respect to time, $\sum\limits_{i=1}^{n} \frac{1}{2} p_i^2 = k$. Hence, $\sum\limits_{i=1}^{n} p_i^2 = 2k$, which is the equation of a sphere.
                                                                    Q.E.D.

THEOREM 4. *There is at least one equilibrium point* $\mathbf{p}^* > 0$ *on each sphere.*

Proof: Let us define the vector function f:

$$f(\mathbf{p})_i = \max \, (p_i + z_i(\mathbf{p}), \tfrac{1}{2} p_i).$$

Let P be the cone of vectors such that $p_i \geq 0$ and $\mathbf{p} \cdot \mathbf{p} \leq 1$. Let $\lambda(\mathbf{p}) = \sqrt{f(\mathbf{p}) \cdot f(\mathbf{p})}$. $f(\mathbf{p})_i \geq \frac{1}{2} p_i$ and $f(\mathbf{p})_i \geq z_i(\mathbf{p})$. If $p_i \neq 0$, then the former is positive; if $p_i = 0$, then the latter is positive by (6). Thus $f(\mathbf{p}) > \mathbf{0}$ on P. Hence the transformation

$$\mathbf{p} \to \frac{f(\mathbf{p})}{\lambda(\mathbf{p})}$$

is well defined and continuous on P. It clearly maps P into P. Hence by the fixed point theorem (see Appendix A) there is a vector $\mathbf{p}^*$ in P such that

$$\mathbf{p}^* = \frac{f(\mathbf{p}^*)}{\lambda(\mathbf{p}^*)}.$$

But $f(\mathbf{p}) > 0$ and $f(\mathbf{p})/\lambda(\mathbf{p})$ has length one always, hence $\mathbf{p}^* > 0$ and $\mathbf{p}^* \cdot \mathbf{p}^* = 1$.

Secondly, we verify that $\lambda(\mathbf{p}^*)$ is actually greater than $\frac{1}{2}$. It could be equal to $\frac{1}{2}$ only if $f(\mathbf{p}^*)_i = \frac{1}{2} p_i^*$ for every i, but then $z_i(\mathbf{p}^*) < 0$ for every i, and hence $\mathbf{p}^* \cdot \mathbf{z}(\mathbf{p}^*) < 0$, contrary to Theorem 2.

But this means that no component p_i^* is equal to $[\frac{1}{2} p_i^*]/\lambda(\mathbf{p}^*)$, and so $f(\mathbf{p}^*) = \mathbf{p}^* + \mathbf{z}(\mathbf{p}^*)$. Hence $\mathbf{p}^* = [\mathbf{p}^* + \mathbf{z}(\mathbf{p}^*)]/\lambda(\mathbf{p}^*)$. If we multiply this equation by $\mathbf{z}(\mathbf{p}^*)$ and use Theorem 2, we obtain $\mathbf{z}(\mathbf{p}^*) \cdot \mathbf{z}(\mathbf{p}^*) = 0$. Hence $\mathbf{z}(\mathbf{p}^*) = 0$, and $\mathbf{p}^*$ is an equilibrium point.

By (5), $\mathbf{z}(c\mathbf{p}^*) = 0$, hence $c\mathbf{p}^*$ is an equilibrium point on the sphere $\mathbf{p} \cdot \mathbf{p} = c^2$.

Q.E.D.

We turn now to the study of the stability of the market. We shall see by an example that not every market is stable. Hence, to obtain stability it is necessary to impose an additional condition. For example:

CONDITION A. For any equilibrium price vector $\bar{\mathbf{p}}$ and any nonequilibrium price vector $\mathbf{p}$, $\bar{\mathbf{p}} \cdot \mathbf{z}(\mathbf{p}) > 0$.

Before examining the consequences of Condition A we shall show that it is satisfied for an important class of market situations.

THEOREM 5. *If the total demands for the entire market may be thought of as arising from maximizing a single utility function u, then Condition A holds.*

Proof: Consider two price vectors $\mathbf{p}$ and $\mathbf{p}'$, and let $\mathbf{x} = \sum_{k=1}^{m} \mathbf{x}^{(k)}$ represent the total demands on the market, and let $\mathbf{x}'$ be the corresponding vector sum when $x_i^{(k)}$ is evaluated by k under the price schedule $\mathbf{p}'$. We assume that $\mathbf{x} \neq \mathbf{x}'$, which will be the case when we choose $\mathbf{p}'$ as an equilibrium point and $\mathbf{p}$ as a nonequilibrium point.

If $\mathbf{p} \cdot \mathbf{x}' \leq \mathbf{p} \cdot \mathbf{x}$, then $\mathbf{x}'$ may be substituted for $\mathbf{x}$ (as far as cost is concerned). But since $\mathbf{x}$ was selected, it must be preferred, i.e., $u(\mathbf{x}') < u(\mathbf{x})$. If we also had $\mathbf{p}' \cdot \mathbf{x} \leq \mathbf{p}' \cdot \mathbf{x}'$, then we would have $u(\mathbf{x}) < u(\mathbf{x}')$, which is a contradiction. Hence, $\mathbf{p} \cdot \mathbf{x}' \leq \mathbf{p} \cdot \mathbf{x}$ implies that $\mathbf{p}' \cdot \mathbf{x} > \mathbf{p}' \cdot \mathbf{x}'$. Since $\mathbf{z}$ differs from $\mathbf{x}$ by a fixed amount, namely $\sum_{k=1}^{m} \mathbf{y}^{(k)}$, we may also state this in terms of $\mathbf{z}$:

If $\mathbf{p} \cdot \mathbf{z}' \leq \mathbf{p} \cdot \mathbf{z}$,   then $\mathbf{p}' \cdot \mathbf{z} > \mathbf{p}' \cdot \mathbf{z}'$.

If we apply Theorem 2, remembering that $\mathbf{z} = \mathbf{z}(\mathbf{p})$, and $\mathbf{z}' = \mathbf{z}(\mathbf{p}')$, we obtain:

$$\text{If } \quad \mathbf{p} \cdot \mathbf{z}(\mathbf{p}') \leq 0, \quad \text{then} \quad \mathbf{p}' \cdot \mathbf{z}(\mathbf{p}) > 0.$$

In particular, if $\mathbf{p}'$ is an equilibrium vector, then $\mathbf{z}(\mathbf{p}') = 0$; hence $\mathbf{p} \cdot \mathbf{z}(\mathbf{p}') \leq 0$ trivially. Therefore, $\mathbf{p}' \cdot \mathbf{z}(\mathbf{p}) > 0$.

Q.E.D.

A second important class of market situations where Condition A is satisfied is that of gross substitution.

CONDITION B (Condition of gross substitution). If the price for one good increases and the other prices remain fixed, then the demand for each of the other goods increases. Mathematically stated (see Appendix F), the partial derivative of z_i with respect to p_j is positive if $i \neq j$.

Under this condition it has been proved that Condition A is satisfied. Also in this case there is a unique equilibrium point on each sphere. We shall not prove these facts.

We return now to the consequences of Condition A.

THEOREM 6. *The set Q of equilibrium vectors is convex under Condition A.*

Proof: Let $\mathbf{p}$ and $\mathbf{q}$ be any two elements of Q and let $\mathbf{r} = \lambda\mathbf{p} + (1 - \lambda)\mathbf{q}$ with $0 < \lambda < 1$. Then if $\mathbf{r}$ is not an equilibrium vector and if Condition A is satisfied, we have $\mathbf{p} \cdot \mathbf{z}(\mathbf{r}) > 0$ and $\mathbf{q} \cdot \mathbf{z}(\mathbf{r}) > 0$. Hence $\mathbf{r} \cdot \mathbf{z}(\mathbf{r}) = \lambda\mathbf{p} \cdot \mathbf{z}(\mathbf{r}) + (1 - \lambda)\mathbf{q} \cdot \mathbf{z}(\mathbf{r}) > 0$, which contradicts Theorem 2. Hence $\mathbf{r}$ is an equilibrium vector. (See Appendix A, Definition 3.)

Q.E.D.

We turn next to the question of stability. We shall assume that our initial price vector $\mathbf{p} = \mathbf{p}(0)$ is not an equilibrium price vector. Let $\mathbf{p}(t)$ be the trajectory. We wish first to consider the distance of this vector from an arbitrary equilibrium vector $\overline{\mathbf{p}}$. This distance is $\sqrt{(\mathbf{p}(t) - \overline{\mathbf{p}}) \cdot (\mathbf{p}(t) - \overline{\mathbf{p}})}$. We wish to show that under Condition A this distance decreases with time. For this purpose it is more convenient to show the equivalent fact that the square of the distance decreases. Therefore we introduce

$$D(t) = (\mathbf{p}(t) - \overline{\mathbf{p}}) \cdot (\mathbf{p}(t) - \overline{\mathbf{p}}).$$

THEOREM 7. *Under Condition A, (i) for any equilibrium vector $\overline{\mathbf{p}}$ and nonequilibrium $\mathbf{p}(t)$, $dD/dt < 0$; and (ii) the market is stable.*

Proof: Differentiating $D(t)$ we have

$$dD/dt = 2(\mathbf{p}(t) - \overline{\mathbf{p}}) \cdot d\mathbf{p}/dt = 2(\mathbf{p}(t) - \overline{\mathbf{p}}) \cdot \mathbf{z}(\mathbf{p})$$
$$= -2\overline{\mathbf{p}} \cdot \mathbf{z}(\mathbf{p})$$

where we have made use of (3') and Theorem 2. Hence (i) follows from Condition A.

If we start with $\mathbf{p}(0)$ as an equilibrium point, then the prices remain at $\mathbf{p}(0)$ forever. Hence, let us suppose that we start with a nonequilibrium price vector $\mathbf{p}(0)$, and let $\bar{\mathbf{p}}$ be any equilibrium point. Since $D \geq 0$ and is monotone decreasing for all time, it tends to a non-negative limit. And since the total change in D is finite, the rate of change dD/dt must tend to 0 along a suitable sequence of points t_n. Hence,

$$(7) \qquad \lim_{t_n \to \infty} \bar{\mathbf{p}} \cdot \mathbf{z}(\mathbf{p}(t_n)) = 0.$$

Since the values of $\mathbf{p}(t_n)$ lie in a closed and bounded set, there must be a convergent subsequence of values $\mathbf{p}(t_n')$. (See Appendix A.) Let us say

$$(8) \qquad \lim_{n \to \infty} \mathbf{p}(t_n') = \mathbf{p}^*.$$

Then, by (4) and (7),

$$\bar{\mathbf{p}} \cdot z(\mathbf{p}^*) = \lim_{n \to \infty} \bar{\mathbf{p}} \cdot \mathbf{z}(\mathbf{p}(t_n')) = 0.$$

Hence, by condition A, $\mathbf{p}^*$ is an equilibrium point. But then we may apply result (i): The distance between $p(t)$ and p^* is monotone decreasing, and for the subsequence of times t_n' it tends to 0. Hence, the distance between $\mathbf{p}(t)$ and $\mathbf{p}^*$ must tend to 0, and so $\mathbf{p}^* = \lim_{t \to \infty} \mathbf{p}(t)$. This establishes (ii).

Q.E.D.

4. Markets with two goods. If there are only two kinds of goods traded in the market, then we can characterize the trajectory exactly, even without assuming Condition A. Since, by (5), $\mathbf{z}$ depends only on the ratio of prices, we introduce the new variable

$$(9) \qquad r = p_2/p_1.$$

Then $z_2(\mathbf{p})$ the second co-ordinate of $\mathbf{z}$ is a function of r, say $z_2(\mathbf{p}) = f(r)$. From Theorem 2 we then find $z_1(\mathbf{p}) = -rf(r)$. Hence

$$(10) \qquad \frac{dr}{dt} = \frac{p_1 \dfrac{dp_2}{dt} - p_2 \dfrac{dp_1}{dt}}{p_1{}^2} = \frac{f(r) + r^2 f(r)}{p_1}.$$

And $p_1{}^2 + p_2{}^2 = c^2, c > 0$. From (9), $p_2 = rp_1$; hence $p_1{}^2(1 + r^2) = c^2$ or

$$(11) \qquad p_1 = \frac{c}{\sqrt{1 + r^2}}; \quad p_2 = \frac{cr}{\sqrt{1 + r^2}}, \quad \text{and}$$

$$(12) \qquad \frac{dr}{dt} = \frac{1}{c}(1 + r^2)^{3/2} f(r).$$

Thus the trajectory lies on the quarter-circle:

$$(13) \qquad p_1{}^2 + p_2{}^2 = c^2, \quad p_1 > 0, p_2 > 0,$$

and its motion is described by (12). We must still find its direction of motion.
The sign of $\dfrac{dr}{dt}$ is the same as that of $f(r)$. Because of (6), if p_2 is near 0, r is near
0, and $f(r) > 0$. If p_1 is near 0, r is very large, and $-rf(r)$ must be positive.
Hence,

(14)   for small r, $f(r) > 0$;   for very large r, $f(r) < 0$.

The first consequence is that $f(r)$ must be 0 at least once, thus yielding at
least one equilibrium point on the circle, verifying Theorem 4. To simplify
the discussion we shall assume that all roots of $f(r)$ are simple.

We must distinguish equilibrium points of the two types shown in
Figure 6.

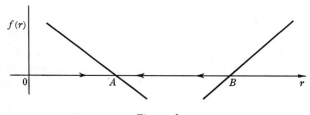

Figure 6

At point A, $f(r)$ goes from $+$ to $-$, at B from $-$ to $+$. Whenever $f(r) > 0$,
$\dfrac{dr}{dt} > 0$; hence, motion is in the direction of increasing r; for $f(r) < 0$,
motion is to the left. Thus, if the trajectory starts near A, it must move
towards A. But we know that A cannot be reached (see Chapter III);
hence, A is approached asymptotically. But near B motion is away from
B, and so we call A a *stable* and B an *unstable* equilibrium point.

Figure 7 shows the most general possibility (if there are no multiple
roots). If the trajectory starts at an equilibrium point, it stays there. Other-

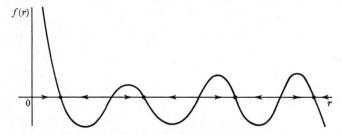

Figure 7   (The solid dots indicate stable equilibrium points.)

wise it moves (asymptotically) towards the neighboring stable equilibrium
point. In any case we see that a market with only two goods is stable.

5. Examples. We shall illustrate the theoretical results by three examples. In the first one Condition A holds; hence, we have stability. In the second one we do not have Condition A, but we have only two goods and hence have stability. The third market is unstable.

EXAMPLE 1. Let us assume that there are only two goods which enter into the trading and that individual k in the market has a utility function of the form

$$(15) \qquad u(x_1,x_2) = a_k \log x_1 + (1 - a_k) \log x_2$$

where $0 < a_k < 1$. The entire market will then have a similar utility function (see Exercise 7). The indifference curves (see Appendix B) for such a utility function are given by

$$a_k \log x_1 + (1 - a_k) \log x_2 = c$$

or

$$x_1{}^{a_k} \cdot x_2{}^{(1-a_k)} = e^c.$$

Thus each individual chooses $\mathbf{x}$ to maximize (15) subject to the constraint $\mathbf{x} \geq 0$ and

$$M^{(k)} = p_1 y_1{}^{(k)} + p_2 y_2{}^{(k)} = p_1 x_1 + p_2 x_2$$

where $\mathbf{y}^{(k)} = (y_1{}^{(k)}, y_2{}^{(k)})$ is his initial endowment. We can find this maximum by replacing x_2 in (15) by $\dfrac{M^{(k)} - p_1 x_1}{p_2}$ and maximizing (15) as a function of one variable. Doing this we obtain the demand function for the kth individual

$$\mathbf{x}^{(k)}(\mathbf{p}) = \left(\frac{a_k M^{(k)}}{p_1}, \frac{(1 - a_k) M^{(k)}}{p_2} \right).$$

Hence,

$$\mathbf{x}^{(k)}(\mathbf{p}) - \mathbf{y}^{(k)} = \left(\frac{p_2}{p_1} a_k y_2{}^{(k)} - (1 - a_k) y_1{}^{(k)}, \frac{p_1}{p_2} (1 - a_k) y_1{}^{(k)} - a_k y_2{}^{(k)} \right).$$

Let $A = \sum_{k=1}^{n} a_k y_2{}^{(k)} > 0$ and $B = \sum_{k=1}^{n} (1 - a_k) y_1{}^{(k)} > 0$, and $r = p_2/p_1$. Then $\mathbf{z}(\mathbf{p}) = (Ar - B, B/r - A)$.

Note that the excess demand function depends only on the ratio r; hence, it is unchanged when the prices are multiplied by a positive constant, verifying (5). As $p_i \to 0$, $z_i(\mathbf{p}) \to +\infty$. Thus (6) holds, but (4) must be modified, as indicated in Section 2.

In order that a price vector $\mathbf{p}$ be an equilibrium price vector we must have $\mathbf{z}(\mathbf{p}) = 0$. That is, $Ar - B = 0$ and $B/r - A = 0$. Both equations are equivalent to

$$(16) \qquad r = p_2/p_1 = B/A.$$

Hence, the equilibrium price vectors are all vectors of the form $\bar{\mathbf{p}} = \lambda(A,B)$ with $\lambda > 0$. Let us compute

$$\bar{\mathbf{p}} \cdot \mathbf{z}(\mathbf{p}) = \lambda A(Ar - B) + \lambda B(B/r - A)$$

$$= \frac{\lambda}{r}(Ar - B)^2 \geq 0.$$

Hence $\bar{\mathbf{p}} \cdot \mathbf{z}(\mathbf{p}) > 0$ if (16) does not hold. This verifies Condition A, and thus Theorem 7 assures stability.

Let us next consider the trajectory. We know that it must lie on a circle, so that

$$(17) \qquad p_1{}^2 + p_2{}^2 = C^2 = p_1(0)^2 + p_2(0)^2.$$

We also know that there is a unique equilibrium point on it. We need only require that $\bar{\mathbf{p}} = (\lambda A, \lambda B)$, then (17) yields $\lambda^2 = C^2/(A^2 + B^2)$; hence,

$$(18) \qquad \bar{\mathbf{p}} = \left(\frac{AC}{\sqrt{A^2 + B^2}}, \frac{BC}{\sqrt{A^2 + B^2}} \right).$$

By stability, for any initial $\mathbf{p}$, the trajectory approaches $\bar{\mathbf{p}}$. Figure 8 shows the trajectory for some typical values. It shows that the change is very rapid when p_2/p_1 is far from the equilibrium value of $B/A = \frac{3}{4}$, but the approach is very slow near this value. This behavior is typical.

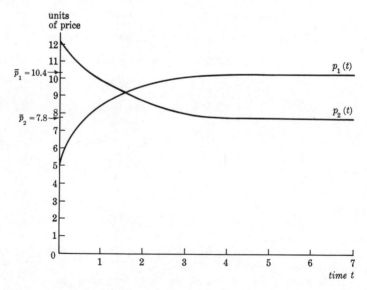

Figure 8   Trajectories for Example 1
$(A = 4, B = 3, \mathbf{p}(0) = (5,12))$

EXAMPLE 2. (Due to L. Hurwicz.) In constructing a demand function it is sometimes more convenient to assume that the person has a utility function for his excess $\mathbf{z}$ rather than for his holdings $\mathbf{x}$. Since we have assumed that he started with an initial endowment $\mathbf{y}$ we are simply considering the utility function

$$\bar{u}(\mathbf{z}) = u(\mathbf{x} - \mathbf{y}).$$

We assume for this example that the utility function for the excess demand of an individual has the form

(19) $$u(\mathbf{z}) = -a_1 e^{-b_1 z_1} - a_2 e^{-b_2 z_2}$$

where a_1, a_2, b_1, b_2 are positive numbers. The individual now maximizes this quantity subject to the constraint

$$p_1 z_1 + p_2 z_2 = 0.$$

When this is carried out the maximum is found to occur for

$$\mathbf{z}(\mathbf{p}) = \left(\frac{r \log cr}{b_2 + b_1 r}, \; -\frac{\log cr}{b_2 + b_1 r} \right),$$

where $c = a_1 b_1 / a_2 b_2$ and $r = p_2/p_1$.

The graph of the excess demand for Good 2 as a function of the price ratio r has the form indicated in Figure 9. The graph crosses the horizontal axis at the point $r = 1/c$. At this point the excess demand for Good 1 is also zero; hence, any prices in this ratio provide equilibrium prices. These are the only such equilibrium prices for the case of a single individual.

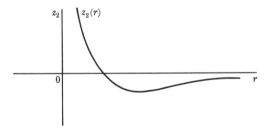

Figure 9 $z_2(r)$ for a single individual

Unlike our previous example, if we consider more than one individual having utility functions of the type (19), then it will no longer be the case that the market utility is of this form. In fact by considering two individuals with different parameter values we can obtain graphs for excess demand for Good 2 of the type indicated in Figure 10. Adding these we obtain a market excess demand for Good 2 as indicated in Figure 11. Since the equilibrium points do not form a convex set, Condition A is violated.

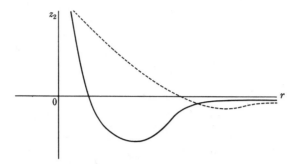

Figure 10 $z_2(r)$ for each individual

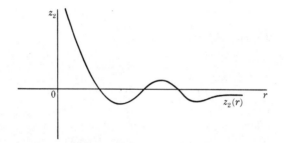

Figure 11 $z_2(r)$ for the market

EXAMPLE 2a. An example of a two person market where the excess demand is of the form indicated in Figure 11 occurs when we choose $c = e^5$, $b_1 = 3$, $b_2 = 1$ for the first individual and $c = e^{-5}$, $b_1 = 1$, $b_2 = 3$ for the second individual. The excess demand is then

$$\mathbf{z}(r) = \left[\frac{r[5 + \log r]}{1 + 3r} + \frac{r[-5 + \log r]}{3 + r}, \; -\frac{[5 + \log r]}{1 + 3r} - \frac{[-5 + \log r]}{3 + r} \right].$$

The graph of the excess demand for Good 2 as a function of the price ratio $r = p_2/p_1$ is given in Figure 12.

We note from this graph that there are three points at which $z_2(\mathbf{p}) = 0$. These occur when $r = .17$, $r = 1$, and $r = 5.89$. As $p_1 z_1(\mathbf{p}) + p_2 z_2(\mathbf{p}) = 0$, we see that at these points we must also have $z_1(\mathbf{p}) = 0$; hence, we have three equilibrium points on each circle.

We consider next the behavior of the market when the process is started out of equilibrium. Let us start with the initial price vector $\mathbf{p}(0) = (1, 1.1)$. For this vector $r = 1.1$; that is, it lies between the second and third equilibrium point. The result is shown in Figure 13. We see that the price vector tends to the third equilibrium point.

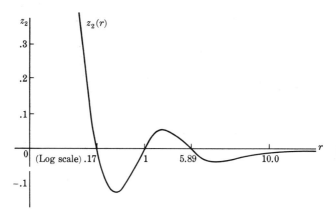

Figure 12 $z_2(r)$ for the market in Example 2a

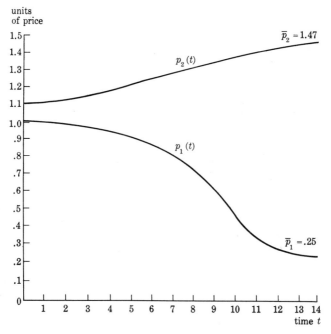

Figure 13 $\mathbf{p}(t)$ for Example 2a where $\mathbf{p}(0) = (1.0, 1.1)$

Consider next the starting vector $\mathbf{p}(0) = (1,10)$. The result of this is shown in Figure 14. Again it is approaching the third equilibrium point. A similar analysis would show that if we start between $r = .17$ and $r = 1$ the price vector will tend towards $r = .17$, and if we start with $r < .17$ it will tend towards $r = .17$. Thus, although $r = 1$ is an equilibrium point, it is an example of an unstable point, whereas the other two points are stable. This illustrates the pattern of alternating stable and unstable equilibrium points found in Section 4.

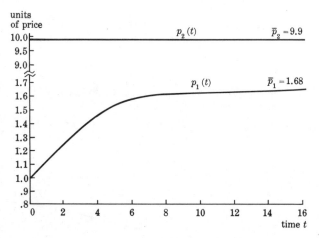

Figure 14 $\mathbf{p}(t)$ for Example 2a where $\mathbf{p}(0) = (1,10)$

EXAMPLE 3. From Section 4 we know that an unstable market must have at least 3 goods. We shall now construct such an example. (This example is due to H. Scarf.)

We shall in this example assume utility functions which do not quite satisfy our conditions for a utility function. We have assumed that our utility functions are strictly convex toward the origin. That is, a line connecting two points of the curve has the property that every point of the curve between the two points lies below the line. We weaken this to require only that no point of the curve lies above the line though it may touch the line. The example can be modified to give a utility function with the strict inequality being satisfied, but the details become much more complicated, and the example below gives the same essential idea as that of the more complicated example.

We assume that there are three individuals in the market. The utility function for the first individual is given by

$$u_1(x_1, x_2, x_3) = \min(x_1, x_2).$$

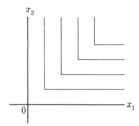

Figure 15   Indifference curves of Goods 1 and 2.

That is, he has no use for Good 3, and his indifference curves for Goods 1 and 2 are as indicated in Figure 15. We assume that his initial amounts of each good are given by

$$\mathbf{y} = (1, 0, 0).$$

It is clear then that for a given price vector $\mathbf{p} = (p_1, p_2, p_3)$ his initial stock is worth p_1. His utility is maximized when he has an equal amount of Good 1 and Good 2. Hence his demand vector for the price vector $\mathbf{p}$ is easily seen to be

$$\mathbf{x}^{(1)}(\mathbf{p}) = \left(\frac{p_1}{p_1 + p_2}, \frac{p_1}{p_1 + p_2}, 0 \right).$$

His excess demand vector will then be

$$\mathbf{z}^{(1)}(\mathbf{p}) = \left(-\frac{p_2}{p_1 + p_2}, \frac{p_1}{p_1 + p_2}, 0 \right).$$

We assume that the second member of the market has the same utility function and initial holding as the first customer except that Good 1 is replaced by Good 2, Good 2 by Good 3, and Good 3 by Good 1; that is, a cyclic permutation is performed on the goods. For the third customer we assume the same behavior except that a further cyclic permutation is performed. The excess demand vectors for the second and third customers are then

$$\mathbf{z}^{(2)}(\mathbf{p}) = \left(0, -\frac{p_3}{p_2 + p_3}, \frac{p_2}{p_2 + p_3} \right),$$

and

$$\mathbf{z}^{(3)}(\mathbf{p}) = \left(\frac{p_3}{p_3 + p_1}, 0, -\frac{p_1}{p_3 + p_1} \right);$$

hence, the market excess demand is

$$\mathbf{z}(\mathbf{p}) = \left(-\frac{p_2}{p_1 + p_2} + \frac{p_3}{p_1 + p_3}, \frac{p_1}{p_1 + p_2} - \frac{p_3}{p_2 + p_3}, \frac{p_2}{p_2 + p_3} - \frac{p_1}{p_1 + p_3} \right).$$

We must note that requirement (6) has been weakened. If $p_i = 0$, then $z_i = 0$. This could be taken care of at the cost of greater complexity in the example.

Thus our system of differential equations for price adjustments is

$$\frac{dp_1}{dt} = -\frac{p_2}{p_1 + p_2} + \frac{p_3}{p_1 + p_3},$$

$$\frac{dp_2}{dt} = -\frac{p_3}{p_2 + p_3} + \frac{p_1}{p_1 + p_2},$$

$$\frac{dp_3}{dt} = -\frac{p_1}{p_1 + p_3} + \frac{p_2}{p_2 + p_3}.$$

We know that the solution will have the property that

(20) $$p_1^2(t) + p_2^2(t) + p_3^2(t) = C.$$

For convenience we shall choose the initial price vector such that $C = 3$. There is a unique equilibrium vector, $\mathbf{p} = (1, 1, 1)$.

A simple computation shows further that

$$\frac{dp_1}{dt} p_2 p_3 + \frac{dp_2}{dt} p_1 p_3 + \frac{dp_3}{dt} p_1 p_2 = 0.$$

That is, the solution must also have the property that

$$p_1(t) p_2(t) p_3(t) = K$$

for all t. Hence if we choose our initial price vector such that $K \neq 1$, we see that the solution will have the property that the components are always positive and lie on the sphere (20) but never approach the equilibrium vector $(1, 1, 1)$, since if they did, the product of the prices would approach 1.

The behavior of this example is analogous to that of the first problem of Chapter III. The prices lie on one of infinitely many concentric closed curves around $(1, 1, 1)$, which are circles in first approximation. The choice of the trajectory depends on $\mathbf{p}(0)$. Once chosen, the trajectory is described periodically for all time. Hence the prices oscillate around the equilibrium values forever. These statements can be proved by the methods of Chapter III.

EXERCISES

1. For the case of two goods in Section 4, describe the nature of a trajectory near a double root of $f(r)$. What can you say about the case of roots of higher order?

2. For the case of two goods in Section 4, prove that there is always at least one stable equilibrium point.

3. Verify that the excess demand vector given for Example 1 does maximize the utility, subject to the budget constraint.

4. Verify that $\sum_i (p_i - \bar{p}_i)^2$ is monotone decreasing in Example 1.

5. For Example 2, show that the utility function is decreasing and convex.

6. Verify for Example 2 that the excess demand function given is correct.

7. Show that, in Example 1, the market demand may be considered to arise from maximizing a market utility function.

8. Show that the excess demand function for Example 1 satisfies Condition B, the condition of gross substitution.

9. Show that the excess demand function for Example 2 does not satisfy Condition B.

10. For Example 3 verify that there is a unique equilibrium point.

11. In Example 3 carry out the computation necessary to show that $p_1 p_2 p_3 = K$.

12. In Example 3 show that the product of the prices can be 1 only when **p** is the equilibrium vector and hence that no matter how the system is started out of equilibrium it will remain out of equilibrium.

13. Consider a market with six men and two goods. Four of the men start with amounts c_1, c_2, c_3, and c_4 of Good 1, respectively, and would like to trade these for as much of Good 2 as possible. The other two men start with amounts d_1 and d_2 of Good 2, respectively, and wish to trade these for Good 1. Show that the market has a unique equilibrium point and is stable. Interpret the equilibrium prices.

14. If a man has an amount m of money to spend and has the utility function $u(x_1,x_2) = x_1{}^a x_2{}^b$, and the prices current are $\mathbf{p} = (p_1,p_2)$, what purchase will he make?

15. Consider the market with a single individual, and two goods. Let his given amounts be $\mathbf{y} = (y_1,y_2)$. Show that the one-person market is always stable, and give a geometric interpretation for the equilibrium prices in terms of his indifference curves. What restriction must we place on his utility function to assure that the equilibrium point is unique?

16. Suppose that there is an equilibrium point $\bar{\mathbf{p}}$ such that for each individual k, $\mathbf{x}^{(k)}(\bar{\mathbf{p}}) = \mathbf{y}^{(k)}$, i.e., at the prices $\bar{\mathbf{p}}$ each individual demands to keep his present commodity bundle. Show that the same must then hold for all equilibrium points and that Condition A holds. (*Hint:* Use a style of proof similar to that of Theorem 5.)

17. Show that the choice of a unit of money has an effect only on the rate of convergence, not on the actual outcome. (*Hint:* Show that if we change **p** to $c\mathbf{p}$ and also change t to ct, then (1) to (6) are unaffected.)

18. Assume that in a market there are two goods and three people. Each individual has one unit of each good when the market opens. The utility function for each of the individuals is $u(x_1,x_2) = x_1{}^{1/3} x_2{}^{2/3}$. Using the result

of Exercise 14, find the excess demand for the market and the equilibrium price vectors. Set up the differential equations for the price changes, and without solving decide whether or not the system is stable.

19. In a market there are two individuals. The first has the utility function $u^{(1)}(x_1,x_2) = (\tfrac{1}{2}) \log x_1 + (\tfrac{1}{2}) \log x_2$ and the second has the utility function $u^{(2)}(x_1,x_2) = (\tfrac{1}{3}) \log x_1 + (\tfrac{2}{3}) \log x_2$. Find the equilibrium price vectors and consider the stability of these vectors.

20. Consider a two-person market in which the individuals have utility functions of the form considered in Example 2a. Let the first person's utility function be determined by $c = 2^8$, $b_1 = 1$, $b_2 = 1$, and the second person's by $c = 2^{-10}$, $b_1 = \tfrac{1}{2}$, $b_2 = 2$. Find the equilibrium points and sketch the graph of the excess demand function for Good 2 as a function of the price ratio. (*Hint:* The equilibrium values of r are all integers.)

PROJECT 1

Consider a market in which there are two men and two goods. Suppose that $u^{(1)}(x_1,x_2) = x_1 x_2$ and $u^{(2)}(x_1,x_2) = x_1^2 x_2$. The first person has 10 units of each good, and the second person has 30 units of Good 1 and 15 units of Good 2. As the market opens, Good 1 is priced at 3 dollars and Good 2 at 4 dollars.

Develop this market in detail, illustrating the results of Section 4.

PROJECT 2

Consider a market with three men and three goods. The first person has an amount a of Good 1, and wishes to trade it for as much of Good 2 as possible. The second person has an amount b of Good 2, which he wishes to trade for Good 3. The third person starts with an amount c of Good 3, and wishes to trade for Good 1.

Develop this market in detail, finding all equilibrium points, and studying the nature of the solution $\mathbf{p}(t)$ near an equilibrium point. Interpret the equilibrium prices.

PROJECT 3

Show that while Equations (1) through (6) are influenced only slightly by a change of the monetary unit (see Exercise 17), they are changed essentially by a change of the unit in which Good i is measured. We would like to require that changing $y_i^{(k)}$ to $c y_i^{(k)}$ for all k, and at the same time changing $\mathbf{p}$ to $(1/c)\mathbf{p}$, should have no effect on the equations. Show that this can be achieved, modifying our model, by changing (3) to

$$\frac{dp_i}{dt} = p_i^2 z_i(\mathbf{p}), \quad \text{for all } i.$$

Study this revised model in detail.

REFERENCES

Arrow, K. J., and Hurwicz, L. "On the Stability of the Competitive Equilibrium, I," *Econometrica*, Vol. 26 (October, 1958), pp. 522–552.

Arrow, K. J., Block, H. D., and Hurwicz, L. "On the Stability of the Competitive Equilibrium, II," *Econometrica*, Vol. 27 (1959), pp. 82–109.

Scarf, H. "Some Examples of Global Instability of the Competitive Equilibrium," *International Economic Review*, Vol. 1, No. 3 (Sept., 1960), pp. 157–172.

Uzawa, H. "Walras' Tâtonnement in the Theory of Exchange," *Review of Economic Studies*, Vol. XXVII, No. 3 (1960), pp. 182–94.

Walras, L. *Eléments d'Economie Politique Pure*. Paris et Lausanne, 1926. (Trans. by W. Jaffé as *Elements of Pure Economics*. Homewood, Ill.: Richard D. Irwin, 1954.)

CHAPTER V

A Markov Chain Model in Sociology

1. Statement of the problem. In this chapter we develop a mathematical model to describe a specific type of experiment. The experiment is quite easy to perform and is repeated many times, with the result that certain regularities are observed.

The experiment that we consider was first performed by Asch: A naive subject is seated at the end of a row of seven pretrained confederates of the experimenter. Instructions are read aloud which lead the subject to believe that he is participating in the following experiment on visual perception: On each of a sequence of trials, the eight individuals present are required to choose aloud (and from a distance) that particular one from among three comparison lines which has the same length as a standard line.

For each set of lines, the naive subject's turn to choose comes only after he has heard the unanimous, though incorrect, responses of the seven confederates. Thus, he is motivated, on the one hand, to answer according to his perceptions and, on the other, to conform to the unanimous choice of the group.

The data for the experiment consist of a sequence of responses for each subject, each response being either a conforming or a nonconforming response.

It is clear that in an experiment like this there is no hope of constructing a mathematical model which predicts exactly what the subject will do on each trial. However, it is possible to construct a probabilistic model which predicts certain average properties of the data and some relations between observable quantities. We shall consider the problem of developing such a model.

The data for testing our model come from a series of experiments carried out by B. Cohen. Each of 33 subjects was exposed to 35 trials. Choices were recorded as a if the subject gave the correct answer, or b if he conformed to the opinion expressed by the stooges. For example, one subject reacted as follows:

$$aaabbaaabbbaaaabaaaaaaaaaaaaaaaaaaa$$

$$\underbrace{\qquad\qquad\qquad\qquad}_{\text{initial segment}} \quad \underbrace{\qquad\qquad\qquad\qquad\qquad}_{\text{final segment}}$$

Figure 16

We define as the *terminal response* the response (a or b) on the 35th trial, and as the *final segment* the sequence of those consecutive responses—ending at the 35th—which are the same as the terminal response. The earlier responses form the *initial segment*. It was not unusual to find fairly long final segments in the data, and occasionally the entire sequence was the final segment.

What quantities can we observe conveniently in such a series of trials? We will start by counting transitions: Let n_{aa} be the number of transitions from a to a in the initial segment, n_{ab} the number of transitions from a to b, and let n_{ba} and n_{bb} be defined similarly. These quantities are well defined except for the first response, which, for example, could be classified either as an a–a or a b–a transition in Figure 16. For reasons that will become clear later, we will count it as an a–a transition. Hence in the sequence in Figure 16, $n_{aa} = 8$, $n_{ab} = 3$, $n_{ba} = 3$, $n_{bb} = 3$.

We choose the first response to be a–a in conformity with our eventual model, which assumes that initially the subject has an a attitude; i.e., that he is inclined to give the right answer. Thus we modify the initial segment by adding a "0-th response" which is an a. Our modified initial segment is shown in Figure 17.

$$aaaabbaaabbbaaaab$$

Figure 17

A number of other easily observable quantities may be deduced from knowledge of the four given n's. For example, if n_a is the total number of times that an a response is given in the (modified) initial segment, and n_b is the total number of b responses, then we have the following relations:

$$n_a = n_{aa} + n_{ab}, \quad n_b = n_{ba} + n_{bb},$$

(1) $$\text{length of initial segment} = n_a + n_b,$$

$$\text{length of final segment} = 36 - (n_a + n_b).$$

To know the total number of a responses we need only one additional piece of information, namely, the terminal response. But that, too, is deducible. If $n_{ab} = n_{ba}$, then the terminal response must be a, whereas if $n_{ab} = n_{ba} + 1$, then the terminal response is b. All of these relations may be established by elementary logical arguments.

Actually, we will not be interested in numbers dealing with a single subject; rather, our concern will be with the data of all 33 subjects. Thus, we will, from now on, let n_{aa} be the total number of a–a transitions in the (modified) initial segments of all subjects. The remaining quantities will be defined similarly. The first two relations in (1) still hold, but n_a is now the total of all a responses in all initial segments, n_b the total of b responses, and their sum is the total length of all initial segments. For these totals there are three more interesting quantities: n is the number of subjects ($n = 33$ in our data), t_a is the number of a terminal responses, and t_b is the number of b terminal responses. From previous remarks we see that

$$(2) \qquad t_b = n_{ab} - n_{ba}, \quad t_a = n - t_b.$$

It will be the task of our model to describe and predict such observational quantities. In one of Cohen's experiments, it was found that

$$(3)$$
$$n_{aa} = 196, \quad n_{ab} = 117, \quad n_{ba} = 106, \quad n_{bb} = 102,$$
$$n_a = 313, \quad n_b = 208, \quad t_a = 22, \quad t_b = 11, \quad n = 33.$$

We shall discuss a model that is designed to make predictions concerning the possible outcomes of such experiments. What kind of predictions should we expect? Since the choice of n, i.e., of the number of subjects, is completely arbitrary, and since outcomes vary greatly from subject to subject, our goal will be the prediction of average values, such as t_b/n and n_{aa}/n. Our model will allow the calculation of the mean values of these averages, and the calculations should be as good as any mean value for the prediction of actual outcomes. In other words, we expect the predictions to differ from actual observations only within precisely calculable bounds, and we expect better agreement as n is increased.

Our procedure will be one common in science. We shall formulate a certain model, without attempting to state how it was originally found. From the model we shall derive a variety of consequences, which are testable by means of the given data. The model will then be judged solely on whether the predictions are in good agreement with observations. It is important to keep this in mind. For example, in describing the model certain intuitively suggestive names will be applied, such as "mental state," or "temporary conforming"; however, the value of the model will in no way be affected by the reasonableness of these names.

2. Mathematical formulation. Let us now describe the model proposed by Cohen for the type of experiment described in Section 1. He assumes that a subject on any one trial may be in one of four mental states:

> State 1: Nonconforming
> State 2: Temporary Nonconforming
> State 3: Temporary Conforming
> State 4: Conforming

The model assumes that the subject starts in State 2. On successive trials it is assumed that the changes in state can be described by a four state

Markov chain (see Appendix C) with transition matrix of the form

$$P = \begin{array}{c} 1 \\ 2 \\ 3 \\ 4 \end{array} \begin{array}{cccc} 1 & 2 & 3 & 4 \\ \left(\begin{array}{cccc} 1 & 0 & 0 & 0 \\ p_{21} & p_{22} & p_{23} & 0 \\ 0 & p_{32} & p_{33} & p_{34} \\ 0 & 0 & 0 & 1 \end{array} \right) \end{array}.$$

Note that transitions from 2 to 4 and from 3 to 1 are excluded. States 1 and 4 cannot be left, and hence are absorbing states. Since it is possible to reach these states from States 2 and 3, we have a four state absorbing Markov chain.

It is assumed that when the subject is in State 1 or 2 he gives a non-conforming response a, and when he is in State 3 or 4 he gives a conforming response b. When an experiment is performed, the experimenter is not able to observe the states of this chain, but only whether the subject conforms or does not conform.

Thus we know that, for the observed sequence of responses in Figure 17, the mental states were as in Figure 18, but we do not know just where in the final segment the subject reached State 1.

$$2222332223333222223(2\ldots 1)$$

Figure 18

Since the chain is an absorbing chain, we know that (given enough time) the subject must reach State 1 or State 4, i.e., be absorbed. It is implicit in our treatment of the final segment that we assume that 35 trials is enough time for each of our subjects to be absorbed.

3. Mathematical treatment. We may now employ Markov chain theory to deduce from our model the mean values of various observed quantities. (See Appendix C.) First of all, we shall put our transition matrix in canonical form by listing the absorbing states first:

$$P = \left(\begin{array}{c|c} I & O \\ \hline R & Q \end{array} \right) = \begin{array}{c} 1 \\ 4 \\ 2 \\ 3 \end{array} \begin{array}{cc} 1 & 4 \\ \left(\begin{array}{cc|cc} 1 & 0 & 0 & 0 \\ 0 & 1 & 0 & 0 \\ \hline p_{21} & 0 & p_{22} & p_{23} \\ 0 & p_{34} & p_{32} & p_{33} \end{array} \right) \end{array}.$$

The fundamental matrix is

$$N = (I - Q)^{-1} = \begin{pmatrix} 1 - p_{22} & -p_{23} \\ -p_{32} & 1 - p_{33} \end{pmatrix}^{-1}.$$

Hence,

$$N = \begin{matrix} 2 \\ 3 \end{matrix} \begin{pmatrix} \dfrac{1-p_{33}}{\Delta} & \dfrac{p_{23}}{\Delta} \\[2mm] \dfrac{p_{32}}{\Delta} & \dfrac{1-p_{22}}{\Delta} \end{pmatrix} = \left(\dfrac{1}{\Delta}\right)\begin{pmatrix} 1-p_{33} & p_{23} \\ p_{32} & 1-p_{22} \end{pmatrix},$$

where

$$\Delta = (1-p_{22})(1-p_{33}) - p_{23}p_{32}.$$

The matrix of absorption probabilities is $B = NR$. Hence,

$$B = NR = \begin{matrix} 2 \\ 3 \end{matrix} \begin{pmatrix} \dfrac{p_{21}(1-p_{33})}{\Delta} & \dfrac{p_{23}p_{34}}{\Delta} \\[2mm] \dfrac{p_{32}p_{21}}{\Delta} & \dfrac{p_{34}(1-p_{22})}{\Delta} \end{pmatrix}$$

$$= \left(\dfrac{1}{\Delta}\right)\begin{pmatrix} p_{21}(1-p_{33}) & p_{23}p_{34} \\ p_{32}p_{21} & p_{34}(1-p_{22}) \end{pmatrix}.$$

Thus, for example, if we start in State 2 the probability of absorption in State 4, i.e., the probability of the subject eventually giving conforming responses, is

$$b_{24} = \frac{p_{23}p_{34}}{\Delta},$$

and $b_{21} = 1 - b_{24}$.

Since the process starts in State 2, according to our model, the entry n_{23} of N gives the mean of the total number of times that the subject is in Mental State 3 during a sequence of trials. Let f_{23} be the mean of the number of times in State 3 in the final segment; then

(4) $\mathbf{M}[n_b/n] = n_{23} - f_{23},$

where $\mathbf{M}[f]$ is the mean of function f, and n_b/n is the average number of b responses per subject in the initial segments. Let q_m be the probability that there are exactly m occurrences of State 3 in the final segment. There will be no such occurrence if the terminal state is 1; hence,

$$q_0 = b_{21}.$$

A simple probabilistic computation will show that

$$q_{m+1} = p_{33}q_m \quad \text{if } m > 0.$$

Hence,

$$q_{m+1} = p_{33}^m q_1.$$

Since

$$1 = \sum_{m=0}^{\infty} q_m = b_{21} + \frac{q_1}{1 - p_{33}},$$

we have

$$q_1 = (1 - p_{33})b_{24}$$

and

$$q_m = p_{33}^{m-1}(1 - p_{33})b_{24}.$$

Hence,

$$f_{23} = \sum_{m=1}^{\infty} m p_{33}^{m-1}(1 - p_{33})b_{24}$$

$$= \frac{b_{24}}{1 - p_{33}} = \frac{p_{23}p_{34}}{\Delta(1 - p_{33})}.$$

And thus, from (4),

(5) $$\mathbf{M}[n_b/n] = \frac{p_{23}}{\Delta} - \frac{p_{23}p_{34}}{\Delta(1 - p_{33})} = \frac{p_{23}p_{32}}{\Delta(1 - p_{33})}.$$

In an analogous manner, we may write $\mathbf{M}[n_a/n] = n_{22} - f_{22}$. Then, carrying out step by step the exact analogue of the above computation, we see that

(6) $$\mathbf{M}[n_a/n] = \frac{1 - p_{33}}{\Delta} - \frac{p_{21}(1 - p_{33})}{\Delta(1 - p_{22})} = \frac{p_{23}(1 - p_{33})}{\Delta(1 - p_{22})}.$$

From the matrix B we obtain

(7) $$\mathbf{M}[t_b/n] = b_{24} = \frac{p_{23}p_{34}}{\Delta},$$

and also $\mathbf{M}[t_a/n] = b_{21}$. However, the latter follows from (7) and (2), since $b_{21} + b_{24} = 1$. (Starting in State 2, the chain must be absorbed in State 1 or 4.)

So far we have obtained three independent estimates for our observational quantities (5), (6), and (7). To obtain a final one, we introduce a modification in our Markov chain. Suppose that the chain is observed only when a change of state takes place. That is, we keep our four states, but we count as a transition only a step from one state to a different state. We again obtain an absorbing Markov chain, and its transition matrix is

$$\hat{P} = \begin{array}{c} \\ 1 \\ 2 \\ 3 \\ 4 \end{array} \begin{array}{cccc} 1 & 2 & 3 & 4 \\ \left(\begin{array}{cccc} 1 & 0 & 0 & 0 \\ \dfrac{p_{21}}{1 - p_{22}} & 0 & \dfrac{p_{23}}{1 - p_{22}} & 0 \\ 0 & \dfrac{p_{32}}{1 - p_{33}} & 0 & \dfrac{p_{34}}{1 - p_{33}} \\ 0 & 0 & 0 & 1 \end{array} \right). \end{array}$$

The fundamental matrix of this process is

$$\hat{N} = \frac{1}{\Delta} \begin{pmatrix} (1 - p_{22})(1 - p_{33}) & p_{23}(1 - p_{33}) \\ p_{32}(1 - p_{22}) & (1 - p_{22})(1 - p_{33}) \end{pmatrix}.$$

The entry $\hat{n}_{23}$ is the mean of the number of changes from Mental State 2 to Mental State 3. This is the same as the number of changes from response a to response b, since a change from State 2 directly to State 4 is impossible. As a matter of fact, it is also the same as the number of such changes in the initial segment, since an a–b change is necessarily in the initial segment. Hence,

$$(8) \qquad \mathbf{M}_{ab} = \mathbf{M}[n_{ab}/n] = \hat{n}_{23} = \frac{p_{23}(1 - p_{33})}{\Delta}.$$

We may now obtain the mean of n_{aa}/n from (1), (6), and (8),

$$(9) \qquad \mathbf{M}_{aa} = \mathbf{M}[n_{aa}/n] = \frac{p_{22}p_{23}(1 - p_{33})}{\Delta(1 - p_{22})}.$$

From (2), (7), and (8),

$$(10) \qquad \mathbf{M}_{ba} = \mathbf{M}[n_{ba}/n] = \frac{p_{23}p_{32}}{\Delta}.$$

And finally, from (1), (5), and (10),

$$(11) \qquad \mathbf{M}_{bb} = \mathbf{M}[n_{bb}/n] = \frac{p_{23}p_{32}p_{33}}{\Delta(1 - p_{33})}.$$

We can show that, conversely, the four means in (8)–(11) determine our transition probabilities. Recalling that the sum of the entries of any row of P is 1, we easily verify that

$$
\begin{aligned}
&p_{21} = \mathbf{M}_{ab}(1 - \mathbf{M}_{ab} + \mathbf{M}_{ba})/(\mathbf{M}_{aa} + \mathbf{M}_{ab})(1 + \mathbf{M}_{ba}) \\
&p_{22} = \mathbf{M}_{aa}/(\mathbf{M}_{aa} + \mathbf{M}_{ab}) \\
(12) \quad &p_{23} = \mathbf{M}_{ab}^2/(\mathbf{M}_{aa} + \mathbf{M}_{ab})(1 + \mathbf{M}_{ba}) \\
&p_{32} = \mathbf{M}_{ba}^2/\mathbf{M}_{ab}(\mathbf{M}_{ba} + \mathbf{M}_{bb}) \\
&p_{33} = \mathbf{M}_{bb}/(\mathbf{M}_{ba} + \mathbf{M}_{bb}) \\
&p_{34} = \mathbf{M}_{ba}(\mathbf{M}_{ab} - \mathbf{M}_{ba})/\mathbf{M}_{ab}(\mathbf{M}_{ba} + \mathbf{M}_{bb}).
\end{aligned}
$$

4. Interpretation of results. The key to the interpretation of a probabilistic model is the Law of Large Numbers. It tells us that if an experiment is repeated a large number of times, and if we compute the average of a certain observable quantity, this average will be very likely to be near its predicted mean. Therefore, if the sequence of trials is repeated for a large number of subjects (i.e., n is large), then the value of n_{ab}/n computed from the data should lie near its mean value $\mathbf{M}_{ab}$ given in (8), and similarly for

M_{aa}, M_{ba}, and M_{bb}. We make a connection between theory and data by assuming that the averages are exactly equal to the predicted means. This enables us to compute the theoretical transition matrix P.

From the data in (3) and the definitions of the M's, the "observed values" are

(13) $\quad M_{aa} = {}^{196}\!/_{33}, \quad M_{ab} = {}^{117}\!/_{33}, \quad M_{ba} = {}^{106}\!/_{33}, \quad M_{bb} = {}^{102}\!/_{33}.$

Hence, from (12),

(14)
$$P = \begin{pmatrix} 1 & 0 & 0 & 0 \\ .06 & .63 & .31 & 0 \\ 0 & .46 & .49 & .05 \\ 0 & 0 & 0 & 1 \end{pmatrix}.$$

Therefore, the observed data allow us to estimate the transition probabilities of our model; we have completed our model on the basis of observations. We must now test the model by making predictions concerning the outcome of experiments and seeing how well these predictions agree with our data.

We could, of course, use Formulas (5) through (11) to predict the means of various observable quantities. Indeed, this could be used to predict outcomes of an additional set of experiments. But it would yield nothing new for the given data, since our P was designed so as to yield the correct values of n_{aa}, n_{ab}, n_{ba}, and n_{bb}, and the other quantities are determined by these. We must, therefore, predict some additional quantities.

Let us make some predictions concerning the number of times that the subject switches responses (from correct to incorrect, or vice versa). The mean number of such switches is $M_{ab} + M_{ba}$; hence it is not new. However, we can also compute the probability of exactly k switches (see Exercises 7 and 8). We show in Table 1 the comparison of observation and prediction.

k	NUMBER OF SUBJECTS WHO SWITCHED k TIMES	PREDICTED NUMBER
0	10	5.22
1	1	2.61
2 or 4	5	7.01
3 or 5	4	3.51
6, 8, or 10	2	5.41
7, 9, or 11	1	2.71
Larger even no.	5	4.30
Larger odd no.	5	2.15

Table 1

Since the numbers for larger k are rather small, we have combined cases. However, we have kept even and odd k separate, since an even k represents a terminal a response, whereas an odd k represents a terminal b response. We see from Table 1 that the predictions are not completely unreasonable, but they tend to underestimate the number of $k = 0$ cases and the number of high k-values. Indeed, if we apply a standard statistical test known as the χ^2-test, we find that in more than 99 per cent of such cases the predictions could be expected to be in better agreement than in Table 1. We are therefore led to reject this model, as not being in sufficiently good agreement with the observed data.

5. An improved model. The usefulness of a precise mathematical model is shown by our ability to demonstrate its shortcomings numerically. And the same reasoning that led us to reject the Cohen model in its original form will lead us to a fairly obvious modification. The major discrepancy in Table 1 is that the model underestimates badly the number of subjects who never switch their response from an a (or correct) response.

This suggests that there may be a significant minority of subjects to whom the model does not apply in that they refuse to be intimidated by the unanimous action of stooges. Let us modify the Cohen model by adding the assumption that some 20 per cent of subjects are of this type, and that the original model is applicable only to the remaining ones. Specifically, we will assume that in his sample seven men fell into this category and we shall apply our computations of Section 3 only to the remaining twenty-six.

If a subject never switches his response, his entire sequence of responses consists of a final segment. Thus his answers do not contribute to the n's computed from initial segments, and hence n_{aa}, n_{ab}, n_{ba}, and n_{bb} are as in (3), but n is reduced to 26. This changes only the denominators in (13), and we obtain as our modified transition matrix

$$(14') \qquad P' = \begin{pmatrix} 1 & 0 & 0 & 0 \\ .04 & .63 & .33 & 0 \\ 0 & .46 & .49 & .05 \\ 0 & 0 & 0 & 1 \end{pmatrix}.$$

We can use this P' to recompute the figures for the expected number of switches. Recalling that seven subjects have been removed, we obtain Table 2.

We immediately see that these predictions are in much better agreement with our observed data. If we apply a χ^2-test again, we find that our deviations are well within the margin of error expected for the worst in 95 per cent of such cases. Hence, we decide that our present model is in reasonable agreement with the observations recorded in the Cohen experiments. Of course, further experimentation is very likely to refute this modified model as well, and to lead in turn to a more sophisticated approach.

k	NUMBER OF SUBJECTS WHO SWITCHED k TIMES	PREDICTED NUMBER
0	3	2.95
1	1	2.16
2 or 4	5	4.27
3 or 5	4	3.13
6, 8, or 10	2	3.74
7, 9, or 11	1	2.75
Larger even no.	5	4.01
Larger odd no.	5	2.94

Table 2

EXERCISES

1. An experiment with thirty subjects yielded the following results: $n_{aa} = 120$, $n_{ab} = 140$, $n_{ba} = 120$, $n_{bb} = 114$.

(a) Estimate the transition matrix P.

(b) Check your answer by means of Formulas (8) through (11).

(c) What is the probability of a subject ending up conforming?

2. Repeat Exercise 1, changing n_{ab} to 150.

3. In an experiment with forty subjects data were collected, and the following transition matrix was arrived at:

$$P = \begin{pmatrix} 1 & 0 & 0 & 0 \\ \frac{7}{36} & \frac{10}{17} & \frac{49}{36} & 0 \\ 0 & \frac{24}{49} & \frac{3}{7} & \frac{4}{49} \\ 0 & 0 & 0 & 1 \end{pmatrix}.$$

What were the observed values of n_{aa}, n_{ab}, n_{ba}, n_{bb}, t_a, and t_b?

4. Compute the mean time to absorption from N, and express it in terms of the **M**'s.

5. (a) Compute the average length of the initial segments for the data in (13).

(b) Use the result of Exercise 4 to compute the mean time to absorption from the data in (13).

(c) Account for the discrepancy in the answers to (a) and (b).

6. (a) Use the result of Exercise 4 to show that the mean time to absorption is always greater than the mean length of the initial segments.

(b) Find a simple expression for the difference in terms of n's and t's. (*Hint:* Use (2).)

(c) Give a probabilistic interpretation of your result.

7. Find the probability that the subject never switches his response (i.e., that he always gives the correct response), and find the probability that he switches exactly once (i.e., that once he begins to conform he continues to conform).

8. Show that the probability of exactly $2k$ switches in response is $[p_{21}/(1 - p_{22})] \cdot [p_{23}p_{32}/(1 - p_{22})(1 - p_{33})]^k$, whereas the probability of exactly $2k + 1$ switches in response is $[p_{23}p_{34}/(1 - p_{22})(1 - p_{33})] \cdot [p_{23}p_{32}/(1 - p_{22})(1 - p_{33})]^k$.

9. Show that the probability of exactly $2k$ or exactly $2k + 1$ switches in response may be estimated by $t_a n_{ba}{}^k/(n_{ab} + t_a)^{k+1}$ and $t_b n_{ba}{}^k/(n_{ab} + t_a)^{k+1}$, respectively.

10. From the results of Exercise 8 compute the probability of an even number of switches, and compare your answer with b_{21}.

11. (a) Estimate the modified transition matrix P' from the data in Exercise 1.

(b) What is the probability that a subject ends up conforming, according to the modified model? (*Hint:* Remember that 20 per cent of the subjects never conform in this model.)

(c) Compare your answers to Exercise 1, Sections (a) and (c).

12. (a) Use the results of Exercise 9 to compute the probability of 0, 2, 4, or 6 switches in response, for the data in Exercise 1.

(b) Carry out the same computation for the modified model. (*Hint:* The results of Exercise 9 are applicable to 80 per cent of the subjects, if t_a is suitably modified.)

(c) Is there a significant difference in the predictions?

PROJECT 1

In the modified model we assumed that 20 per cent of the subjects refuse to be intimidated and hence are certain to make the correct response every time. The Cohen model was then applied to the remaining subjects. Generalize this model by assuming that a fraction p of the subjects refuse to be intimidated, and that the Cohen model is applied to the remaining subjects. Compute for this model the mean value of the quantities needed to estimate the transition matrix. You will need one more quantity, since there is an added parameter p. Use for this the mean number of subjects that always make a correct response. From the observed values of these quantities, obtain p and the new P' for the Cohen experiment, and devise tests for the new model.

PROJECT 2

Let $n_a{}^{(k)}$ be the number of responses of type a in the first k trials of an individual subject. Show that

$$\mathbf{M}_2[n_a{}^{(m)}] = \sum_{j=0}^{m} p_{22}{}^{(j)} + \sum_{j=1}^{m} p_{22}{}^{(j-1)} p_{21}(m - j + 1).$$

Using this, show that

$$\lim_{n \to \infty} [\mathbf{M}_2[n_a{}^{(m)}] - (m + 1)b_{21}] = n_{22} - p_{21}(n_{22}^2 + n_{23}n_{32}).$$

You will have to use the fact that, for any absorbing chain, $N^2 = I + 2Q + 3Q^2 + \cdots$.

Therefore, for large m, $\mathbf{M}_2[n_a{}^{(m)}]$ is approximately

$$(m + 1)b_{21} + n_{22} - p_{21}(n_{22}^2 + n_{23}n_{32}).$$

We may use this to estimate the *total* number of a responses per subject by assuming that the approximation holds for $m = 35$.

In the Cohen experiment the number of a responses per subject was 25.1. Compare the observed average with the predicted value both for the Cohen model and the modified model.

PROJECT 3

Study the following two-parameter model for Asch type experiments. There are four states: 1, 2, 3, 4. These again represent mental states of the subject. When in State 1 he is certain to give a nonconforming response. When in State 2 he conforms with probability $\frac{1}{3}$. When in State 3 he conforms with probability $\frac{2}{3}$, and when he is in State 4 he is certain to conform. The subject moves through these states according to a Markov chain with transition matrix of the form

$$P = \begin{array}{c} \\ 1 \\ 2 \\ 3 \\ 4 \end{array} \begin{array}{c} \begin{array}{cccc} 1 & 2 & 3 & 4 \end{array} \\ \begin{pmatrix} 1 & 0 & 0 & 0 \\ q & r & p & 0 \\ 0 & q & r & p \\ 0 & 0 & 0 & 1 \end{pmatrix} \end{array}.$$

Obtain the mean value of at least two observable quantities and show that p and q may be estimated from these. You may wish to use a quantity like that developed in Project 2.

REFERENCES

Asch, S. E. *Social Psychology*. New York: Prentice-Hall, 1952.

Cohen, B. P. "A Probability Model for Conformity," *Sociometry*, Vol. 21, No. 1 (March, 1958), pp. 69–81.

CHAPTER VI

Stabilization of Money Flow
An Application of Discrete Potential Theory

1. The problem. Let us consider a country with n cities. At the moment our study begins, each city has a certain quantity of currency. This currency flows from city to city. Choosing a convenient unit of time, e.g. one year, we observe that in a given period a certain fraction of the currency at city i is transferred to city j. We may actually imagine a sample of the bills marked, and counted a year later, to see what fraction of them ends up in each city.

If such a flow of currency is unchecked, it can result in a highly unstable situation. For example, several cities may run out of currency, whereas others may end up with much more than they need. We shall consider one type of remedy: The government releases certain sums in various cities, releasing the same amounts in each period, and it removes currency from other cities.

As a goal, it sets itself a fixed distribution of currency that appears to be ideal. It will be required that this goal be approached (in the sense of a limit) as the number of time periods increases.

Of course, not all goals are feasible. Hence, our first task will be to find conditions under which the government can achieve its purpose. Secondly, for feasible goals we must find the right amounts of money to be supplied to (or withdrawn from) each city in each period.

A basic assumption in this problem will be that no money appears from outside the country. We will allow, however, that some of the money in city i should "disappear" during the period. This may represent either the flow of money out of the country or the hoarding of currency by individuals. We will also assume that money from any one city can eventually reach any other city.

After solving this problem, we will consider a harder version. Suppose that the government can manipulate currency only in a subset of the cities. For example, if the government must operate through a federal reserve bank, then only cities with federal reserve banks can be used.

2. Mathematical formulation. We will represent sums of money by row vectors, whose ith component represents city number i. Thereby, $\mathbf{m} = (m_i)$ is the money currently present at the various cities; $\mathbf{f} = (f_i)$ is the money supplied in each period by the government; and $\mathbf{g} = (g_i)$ is the goal the government aims at, i.e., the money they hope to have in circulation after the flow stabilizes. It is clear from the definitions that $\mathbf{m}$ and $\mathbf{g}$ are positive vectors. However, $\mathbf{f}$ may have both positive and negative components. If f_i is positive, then this sum is injected into the economy periodically at city i; whereas if f_i is negative, it indicates money withdrawn from circulation in each period.

Let p_{ij} be the fraction of the money in city i that ends up in city j at the end of one period. Since $0 \le p_{ij} \le 1$, we may think of these as probabilities. This will allow us to apply Markov chain theory (see Appendix C), even though our problem is strictly determined. The "states" of the chain are our cities, i.e., s_i is city number i; whereas the assumption that money from one city can eventually reach any other city assures us that our states "communicate."

If money cannot disappear, we let $P = (p_{ij})$; and since in this case $\sum_j p_{ij} = 1$, the matrix P is a transition matrix of an ergodic chain. If money can disappear, we let $Q = (p_{ij})$, and add an "absorbing city," which is supposed to receive all the disappearing money. (Of course, this innocent fiction is introduced purely as a mathematical convenience.) We then obtain an absorbing chain with one absorbing state.

Let us now consider the distribution of money after n periods. We carry out our computation first for the ergodic case. Of the original sums $\mathbf{m}$, after one time-period $\sum_i m_i p_{ij}$ is at city j. Thus, $\mathbf{m}P$ gives the distribution of money after one period. Similarly, $\mathbf{m}P^2$ gives it after two periods, $\mathbf{m}P^3$ after three, and $\mathbf{m}P^n$ after n time periods.

Similarly we see that the money injected into the economy at the beginning changes this total by $\mathbf{f}P^n$ in n periods. The money supplied in the first period causes a cumulative change of $\mathbf{f}P^{n-1}$, etc. Thus, the total sum available after n periods is

(1)
$$\mathbf{m}P^n + \sum_{k=0}^{n} \mathbf{f}P^k.$$

Since $\mathbf{f}$ is not necessarily positive, we must make sure that this sum never becomes negative at any city, or else our solution is not implementable. Hence one key requirement is that (1) should be non-negative for all n. Subject to this restriction, our aim is to have the quantities (1) converge to $\mathbf{g}$.

The computation for the absorbing case is almost identical. But since we are interested only in the money that stays inside the country, Q plays the role of P in (1), and we are led to

(1')
$$\mathbf{m}Q^n + \sum_{k=0}^{n} \mathbf{f}Q^k.$$

We must again require that these quantities be non-negative for all n, and that they should converge to our goal $\mathbf{g}$.

3. The absorbing case. For an absorbing chain, Q^n tends to 0, and the matrix $N = (I - Q)^{-1} = I + Q + Q^2 + \cdots$ plays a fundamental role.

By examining (1'), we see that the first term tends to 0, whereas the second approaches $\mathbf{f}N$. Thus, if our goal is to be achieved, we want $\mathbf{f}N = \mathbf{g}$. Since $N = (I - Q)^{-1}$, this means

$$(2) \qquad\qquad\qquad \mathbf{f} = \mathbf{g}(I - Q).$$

Thus we see that if $\mathbf{g}$ is feasible, there is a unique $\mathbf{f}$ that will achieve the goal, namely the one given by (2). Furthermore, this $\mathbf{f}$ will achieve the goal as long as the quantities in (1') are non-negative for all n. Replacing $\mathbf{f}$ in (1') from our value in (2), these requirements become

$$\mathbf{m}Q^n + \mathbf{g}(I - Q) \cdot \sum_{k=0}^{n} Q^k = \mathbf{m}Q^n + \mathbf{g}(I - Q^{n+1}) \geq 0$$

or

$$(3) \qquad\qquad\qquad (\mathbf{g}Q - \mathbf{m})Q^n \leq \mathbf{g} \quad \text{for } n \geq 0.$$

This appears at first to be very difficult to enforce, since there are infinitely many conditions. However, we shall see that only a finite number of conditions need to be tested.

THEOREM.

(*i*) *If for some k the sum of the absolute values of the components of $(\mathbf{g}Q - \mathbf{m})Q^k$ is no greater than the least entry of $\mathbf{g}$, then (3) holds for all $n \geq k$; and this must occur for some k.*

(*ii*) *If $(\mathbf{g}Q - \mathbf{m})Q^{k+1} \leq (\mathbf{g}Q - \mathbf{m})Q^k$, and (3) holds for k, then (3) holds for $n \geq k$.*

(*iii*) *If $\mathbf{g}Q \leq \mathbf{g}$, then (3) holds for all n, for all $\mathbf{m}$.*

Proof: Let $\mathbf{h} = (\mathbf{g}Q - \mathbf{m})Q^k$. Then $(\mathbf{g}Q - \mathbf{m})Q^n = \mathbf{h}Q^{n-k}$, and the components of Q to any power are never greater than 1. Hence a component of $\mathbf{h}Q^{n-k}$ is bounded by $\sum |h_i|$. Hence, if as in (*i*)

$$\sum_i |h_i| \leq \min_i g_i,$$

then (3) holds for $n \geq k$, and since $Q^k \to 0$, $\mathbf{h}$ also tends to 0. Hence, $\sum_i |h_i| \leq \min_i g_i$ for sufficiently high k.

If $\mathbf{h}Q \leq \mathbf{h}$, then we can multiply both sides by the non-negative matrix Q^m to obtain $\mathbf{h}Q^{m+1} \leq \mathbf{h}Q^m$, showing that $\mathbf{h}Q^m$ is monotone decreasing. Hence (*ii*) holds. And, similarly, if $\mathbf{g}Q \leq \mathbf{g}$, then $\mathbf{g}Q^{n+1} \leq \mathbf{g}$ for all n; hence (3) holds for all n, even without the term $\mathbf{m}Q^n$. Thus (*iii*) follows.

Q.E.D.

We now have an effective procedure for checking (3) in a finite number of steps. We compute $(\mathbf{g}Q - \mathbf{m})Q^n$ for successive n, starting with $n = 0$. If (3) is violated for any of these, then $\mathbf{g}$ is not feasible. Eventually we reach a vector satisfying the condition in (i), and if (3) has not been violated till this point, it will never be violated; hence $\mathbf{g}$ is feasible. The part (ii) of the Theorem shows us that often we can stop much sooner. Namely, if a vector computed is no greater than the previous one, we may stop. And (iii) shows us that in some cases the entire computation may be omitted. We should note that $\mathbf{g}Q \leq \mathbf{g}$ is precisely the condition that $\mathbf{f} \geq 0$, and in this case the quantities (1') are obviously non-negative. These cases will be illustrated in Section 6.

What is the total amount of money that must be supplied per period, given a feasible $\mathbf{g}$? If $\mathbf{1}$ is the column vector all of whose components are 1, we seek to find $\mathbf{f1}$. This, from (2), is $\mathbf{g}(I - Q)\mathbf{1}$. Let $\mathbf{h} = (I - Q)\mathbf{1} \geq 0$. Then the total amount needed is $\mathbf{gh}$. Thus the column vector $\mathbf{h}$ converts the goal into a requirement on how much money needs to be injected into the economy at each period. Since in the absorbing case money disappears from the system, it is not surprising that $\mathbf{f1} > 0$. It does not mean, however, that $\mathbf{f} \geq 0$, since $\mathbf{g}(I - Q)$ will generally have negative components.

One particularly interesting feature of the solution given in (2) is that $\mathbf{f}$ does not depend on $\mathbf{m}$; namely, on the amounts present at the start.

4. The ergodic case. As we have seen, P is an ergodic transition matrix if $\sum_j p_{ij} = 1$ for all cities i. This means that the system is "conserving," i.e., no money can disappear. The mathematical treatment of ergodic chains is somewhat complicated by the possibility of a "cyclic" structure. However, this is impossible if even a single diagonal entry p_{ii} is positive. Thus we need only assume that in at least one city some part of its money remains within the city for a time period. In practice, this is presumably true for every city. Thus we may safely assume that P is regular.

Let us now study (1) for a regular chain. The first term $\mathbf{m}P^n$ tends to $(\mathbf{m1})\boldsymbol{\alpha}$. Here $\mathbf{m1}$ is a number, namely the total money in circulation at the beginning. Thus, we see that no matter what sums are available at the beginning, these redistribute themselves to amounts proportional to $\boldsymbol{\alpha}$, where the proportionality constant is the total amount of money available.

Let us next examine the second term, the series $\mathbf{f} + \mathbf{f}P + \mathbf{f}P^2 + \cdots$. If this series is to converge, $\mathbf{f}P^n$ must tend to 0. But $\mathbf{f}P^n$ tends to $(\mathbf{f1})\boldsymbol{\alpha}$, and $\boldsymbol{\alpha} \neq 0$. Hence, a necessary condition for convergence is that $\mathbf{f1} = 0$. This means that if the government wishes to achieve stability in a conserving system, the net total money supplied must be 0. That is, for whatever sums are supplied to some of the cities, an equal amount must be withdrawn from others!

Actually, this condition is also sufficient for convergence, for if $\mathbf{f1} = 0$, $\mathbf{f}A = 0$ also. Hence,

$$\mathbf{f} + \mathbf{f}P + \mathbf{f}P^2 + \cdots = \mathbf{f} + \mathbf{f} \sum_{n=1}^{\infty} (P^n - A) = \mathbf{f}Z.$$

Thus for the goal to be achieved we require

(4) $$\mathbf{g} = (\mathbf{m1})\alpha + \mathbf{f}Z.$$

It should be intuitively clear from the above discussion that there must be a restriction on $\mathbf{g}$. Since the net amount of money supplied in each period is 0, and the system is conserving, the total amount after any period must be the same as the original amount. Indeed, since $Z1 = 1$,

(5) $$\mathbf{g1} = (\mathbf{m1})(\alpha1) + \mathbf{f1} = \mathbf{m1}.$$

Let us now solve equation (4), by multiplying by $(I - P + A)$:

$$\mathbf{g}(I - P + A) = (\mathbf{m1})(\alpha - \alpha + \alpha) + \mathbf{f},$$

where we have used $\alpha P = \alpha$, $\alpha A = \alpha$, and $Z = (I - P + A)^{-1}$. Hence, by (5),

(6) $$\mathbf{f} = \mathbf{g}(I - P).$$

We must still check whether $\mathbf{f1} = 0$. But $P1 = 1$; hence, $(I - P)1 = 0$, and thus our requirement is satisfied. We see that $\mathbf{g1} = \mathbf{m1}$ is the necessary and sufficient condition for the existence of an $\mathbf{f}$ such that (1) converges to $\mathbf{g}$. And the only possible $\mathbf{f}$ is given by (6). We must still make sure that the quantities in (1) are never negative.

In exact analogy to (3), we arrive at condition

(3') $$(\mathbf{g}P - \mathbf{m})P^n \leq \mathbf{g} \quad \text{for all } n \geq 0,$$

and the Theorem of Section 3 holds for the ergodic case if we replace Q in that theorem by P. The proof is almost identical with the one given for the absorbing case. We need only modify it by noting that P^n itself does not converge to 0, but $\mathbf{h} = (\mathbf{g}P - \mathbf{m})P^k$ converges to $(\mathbf{g}P - \mathbf{m})A = \mathbf{g}A - \mathbf{m}A$, which is 0 by (5). Thus we can again check the conditions of (3') in a finite number of steps.

The short-cut (ii) of the Theorem is still very useful. However (iii), while still correct, only covers a single case. If $\mathbf{g}$ is positive and $\mathbf{g}P \leq \mathbf{g}$, then it can be shown (see Exercise 19) that $\mathbf{g}$ is a multiple of α, namely $\mathbf{g} = (\mathbf{g1})\alpha$, and hence is $\mathbf{g} = (\mathbf{m1})\alpha$ by (5). This is, of course, achievable; namely, by leaving the system alone $(\mathbf{f} = 0)$.

Whereas in the absorbing case we had to check only (3), in the ergodic case we have to check (3') and (5) to see whether $\mathbf{g}$ is feasible. In both cases, however, for a feasible $\mathbf{g}$ there is a unique $\mathbf{f}$ that achieves the goal—namely, the one given by (2) or (6), respectively.

5. A harder problem. Suppose that the government can step in only at certain select cities. We may as well suppose that these are cities $1, 2, \ldots, k$, since the numbering of cities is arbitrary. This means that $f_i = 0$ for $i > k$. Everything we have computed in the past two sections is still applicable, but we must further restrict the goals. For regular chains we found that the unique possible solution is $\mathbf{f} = \mathbf{g}(I - P)$, and we must now make sure that $\mathbf{f}$ has nonzero components only in the select cities. The necessary computation will be the same for absorbing chains, if P is replaced by Q.

It will be convenient to break up the matrix P into four submatrices, showing the select states:

$$P = \begin{array}{c} \\ \text{select} \\ \text{other} \end{array} \overset{\text{select} \quad \text{other}}{\left(\begin{array}{cc} T & U \\ V & W \end{array} \right)}.$$

Similarly, let $\mathbf{g} = (\mathbf{g}^*, \mathbf{g}^{**})$, with $\mathbf{g}^*$ containing the select components.

$$(7) \qquad \mathbf{g}(I - P) = \begin{cases} \mathbf{g}^* - \mathbf{g}^*T - \mathbf{g}^{**}V & \text{in the select states,} \\ \mathbf{g}^{**} - \mathbf{g}^*U - \mathbf{g}^{**}W & \text{in the other states.} \end{cases}$$

Thus our new condition is

$$\mathbf{g}^{**} - \mathbf{g}^*U - \mathbf{g}^{**}W = 0$$

or

$$\mathbf{g}^{**}(I - W) = \mathbf{g}^*U.$$

It is easily seen that W is the Q-matrix of an absorbing chain; hence $(I - W)$ has an inverse—this inverse being the fundamental matrix of the absorbing chain—and it is a positive matrix. (See Appendix C.) Thus we must require

$$(8) \qquad\qquad \mathbf{g}^{**} = \mathbf{g}^*U(I - W)^{-1}.$$

Therefore, the government has no choice in the values of $\mathbf{g}$ outside the select states; once $\mathbf{g}^*$ is chosen, $\mathbf{g}^{**}$ is determined by (8). We can now compute the non-zero components of $\mathbf{f}$ from (7).

$$\mathbf{f}^* = \mathbf{g}^*(I - T - U(I - W)^{-1}V).$$

Let us define $P^* = T + U(I - W)^{-1}V$. Then

$$(9) \qquad\qquad \mathbf{f}^* = \mathbf{g}^*(I - P^*).$$

Consider the matrix P^*. It is a non-negative matrix, which has an interesting probabilistic interpretation. It is the transition matrix of the Markov chain we obtain if we "watch the original chain only in the select states."

That is, p_{ij}^* is the probability starting in s_i, that the next time the process is in a select state it is at s_j. We can also give it an economic interpretation. Suppose that we mark the currency in city i. We watch each bill until it shows up in a select city, and p_{ij}^* is the fraction of these bills that will show up at j first.

If P was the transition matrix of an ergodic chain, then so is P^*. Hence $P^*\mathbf{1} = \mathbf{1}$, and thus (9) guarantees that $\mathbf{f}^*\mathbf{1} = 0$; and since the components of $\mathbf{f}$ for nonselect states are 0, $\mathbf{f1} = 0$. Therefore, we have solved our problem for this case: $\mathbf{g}$ is feasible if and only if (3'), (5), and (8) are satisfied, and in these cases (9) provides the solution.

In the absorbing case we form Q^* in a manner exactly analogous to the formation of P^* above. Of course, in this case Q^* does not have row sums equal to 1, which corresponds to the fact that from a nonabsorbing state we need not return to any set of nonabsorbing states, since the process may be absorbed before returning. Otherwise the above computation can be repeated. We then find that $\mathbf{g}$ is feasible if and only if (3) and (8) hold, and then the unique solution is

$$(9') \qquad \mathbf{f}^* = \mathbf{g}^*(I - Q^*).$$

The total amount of money that needs to be supplied per period may again be found by letting $\mathbf{h}^* = (I - Q^*)\mathbf{1} > 0$, and $\mathbf{f}^*\mathbf{1} = \mathbf{g}^*\mathbf{h}^*$.

6. Examples. Let us suppose that there are three cities. Cities A and C each keep half their money during a given time period, and ship half the remainder to each of their neighboring cities. On the other hand, City B sends all of its currency out, splitting the sums equally. This furnishes the flow-matrix

$$P = \begin{matrix} & \begin{matrix} A & B & C \end{matrix} \\ \begin{matrix} A \\ B \\ C \end{matrix} & \begin{pmatrix} \tfrac{1}{2} & \tfrac{1}{4} & \tfrac{1}{4} \\ \tfrac{1}{2} & 0 & \tfrac{1}{2} \\ \tfrac{1}{4} & \tfrac{1}{4} & \tfrac{1}{2} \end{pmatrix} \end{matrix}.$$

Since $\boldsymbol{\alpha}$ is characterized by the fact that $\boldsymbol{\alpha}P = \boldsymbol{\alpha}$ and $\boldsymbol{\alpha}\mathbf{1} = 1$, we find that $\boldsymbol{\alpha} = (\tfrac{2}{5}, \tfrac{1}{5}, \tfrac{2}{5})$.

$$I - P + \mathbf{1}\boldsymbol{\alpha} = \begin{pmatrix} \tfrac{9}{10} & -\tfrac{1}{20} & \tfrac{3}{20} \\ -\tfrac{1}{10} & \tfrac{6}{5} & -\tfrac{1}{10} \\ \tfrac{3}{20} & -\tfrac{1}{20} & \tfrac{9}{10} \end{pmatrix},$$

$$Z = \begin{pmatrix} \tfrac{86}{75} & \tfrac{1}{25} & -\tfrac{14}{75} \\ \tfrac{2}{25} & \tfrac{21}{25} & \tfrac{2}{25} \\ -\tfrac{14}{75} & \tfrac{1}{25} & \tfrac{86}{75} \end{pmatrix}.$$

Let us suppose that at the beginning the amounts of money present are $\mathbf{m} = (10, 6, 5)$. The government wishes to equalize the currency in the three cities. Hence, it must choose $\mathbf{g} = (7, 7, 7)$, to keep the total at 21. Then $\mathbf{g}P = (^{35}\!/_4, ^{7}\!/_2, ^{35}\!/_4)$, and

$$\mathbf{f} = \mathbf{g} - \mathbf{g}P = (-^{7}\!/_4, ^{7}\!/_2, -^{7}\!/_4).$$

Thus it must supply $3\frac{1}{2}$ units per period to City B, and withdraw half of this amount from each of the other two cities. We can check, using (4), that $(\mathbf{m}1)\alpha = 21\alpha = (^{42}\!/_5, 21\!/_5, ^{42}\!/_5)$, and $\mathbf{f}Z = (-^{7}\!/_5, ^{14}\!/_5, -^{7}\!/_5)$; and these two vectors do add up to $\mathbf{g}$.

We must still check (3'). We compute:

$$(\mathbf{g}P - \mathbf{m}) = (-^{5}\!/_4, -^{19}\!/_4, ^{15}\!/_4); \quad (\mathbf{g}P - \mathbf{m})P = (-^{15}\!/_{16}, ^{19}\!/_{16}, ^{5}\!/_{16}).$$

Both vectors are below $\mathbf{g}$, and the sum of the absolute values of the components of the second vector is $^{15}\!/_8$, which is less than 7. Hence, by our Theorem, (3') is met.

Now let us suppose that the government can step in only at Cities A and B.

$$T = \begin{pmatrix} \frac{1}{2} & \frac{1}{4} \\ \frac{1}{2} & 0 \end{pmatrix} \quad U = \begin{pmatrix} \frac{1}{4} \\ \frac{1}{2} \end{pmatrix}$$

$$V = (\frac{1}{4} \quad \frac{1}{4}) \quad W = (\frac{1}{2})$$

$$(I - W)^{-1} = (2) \quad U(I - W)^{-1} = \begin{pmatrix} \frac{1}{2} \\ 1 \end{pmatrix} \quad P^* = \begin{pmatrix} ^{5}\!/_8 & ^{3}\!/_8 \\ ^{3}\!/_4 & \frac{1}{4} \end{pmatrix}$$

If $\mathbf{m} = (10, 6, 5)$, then two restrictions on $\mathbf{g} = (g_A, g_B, g_C)$, namely (5) and (8), are

$$g_A + g_B + g_C = 21$$

$$g_C = g_A/2 + g_B.$$

Or equivalently,

(10)

$$g_B = 21/2 - 3g_A/4$$

$$g_C = 21/2 - g_A/4.$$

To make $\mathbf{g} > 0$, g_A may be selected freely as long as $0 < g_A < 14$. Then $\mathbf{g}$ is determined by (10). The solution given by (9), $\mathbf{f}^* = \mathbf{g}^*(I - P^*)$, is

$$f_A = 3g_A/8 - 3g_B/4 = 15g_A/16 - 63/8, \quad \text{and} \quad f_B = -f_A.$$

We have now made sure that (5) and (8) hold, but we must still check (3'). This will further restrict the choice of g_A. (See Exercise 21.)

Thus, if $g_A = 10$ is chosen, then $\mathbf{g} = (10, 3, 8)$, and $\mathbf{f} = (^{3}\!/_2, -^{3}\!/_2, 0)$. As before, $(\mathbf{m}1)\alpha = (^{42}\!/_5, 21\!/_5, ^{42}\!/_5)$; however, now $\mathbf{f}Z = (^{3}\!/_5, -^{6}\!/_5, -^{2}\!/_5)$, and the sum of these two vectors is again $\mathbf{g}$. We must check (3') for this $\mathbf{g}$.

We find that

$$(\mathbf{g}P - \mathbf{m}) = (-\tfrac{3}{2}, -\tfrac{3}{2}, 3); \quad (\mathbf{g}P - \mathbf{m})P = (-\tfrac{3}{4}, \tfrac{3}{8}, \tfrac{3}{8}).$$

Both are below $\mathbf{g}$ and the second has an absolute row-sum of $\tfrac{3}{2}$, which is below the least entry of $\mathbf{g}$. Hence (3′) holds, by our Theorem. Thus $\mathbf{g}$ is feasible.

For an absorbing example we choose

$$Q = \begin{array}{c} \\ A \\ B \\ C \end{array} \begin{array}{ccc} A & B & C \\ \left(\begin{array}{ccc} \tfrac{1}{2} & \tfrac{1}{4} & \tfrac{1}{4} \\ \tfrac{1}{4} & \tfrac{1}{2} & \tfrac{1}{4} \\ 0 & \tfrac{1}{4} & \tfrac{1}{2} \end{array} \right). \end{array}$$

Here $\tfrac{1}{4}$ of the currency in City C flows out of the country in each time period.

To obtain a Markov chain, we add a fictitious absorbing city:

$$P = \begin{array}{c} \\ \text{abs} \\ A \\ B \\ C \end{array} \begin{array}{ccccc} \text{abs} & A & B & C \\ \left(\begin{array}{c|ccc} 1 & 0 & 0 & 0 \\ 0 & \tfrac{1}{2} & \tfrac{1}{4} & \tfrac{1}{4} \\ 0 & \tfrac{1}{4} & \tfrac{1}{2} & \tfrac{1}{4} \\ \tfrac{1}{4} & 0 & \tfrac{1}{4} & \tfrac{1}{2} \end{array} \right). \end{array}$$

$$N = \left(\begin{array}{ccc} 4 & 4 & 4 \\ \tfrac{8}{3} & 16\tfrac{2}{3} & 4 \\ \tfrac{4}{3} & \tfrac{8}{3} & 4 \end{array} \right).$$

If $\mathbf{g} = (12, 8, 20)$, then $\mathbf{f} = \mathbf{g} - \mathbf{g}Q = (4, -4, 5)$. We verify that $\mathbf{f}N = \mathbf{g}$. Thus the government must supply four units in City A, five in City C, and withdraw four in City B, in each period. Whether (3) is satisfied will, of course, depend on the originally available currency $\mathbf{m}$. If $\mathbf{m} = (4, 4, 4)$, then

$$(\mathbf{g}Q - \mathbf{m}) = (4, 8, 11); \quad (\mathbf{g}Q - \mathbf{m})Q = (4, 3\tfrac{1}{4}, 1\tfrac{7}{2}).$$

Since each is below $\mathbf{g}$ and the second vector is less than or equal to the first, (3) follows from the Theorem, part (ii), and $\mathbf{g}$ is feasible. On the other hand, if $\mathbf{m} = (2, 4, 2)$, then

$$(\mathbf{g}Q - \mathbf{m}) = (6, 8, 13); \quad (\mathbf{g}Q - \mathbf{m})Q = (5, 3\tfrac{5}{4}, 10).$$

Hence we note that the second vector violates (3), and thus our $\mathbf{g}$ is *not* feasible for $\mathbf{m} = (2, 4, 2)$.

Let us next consider the goal $\mathbf{g} = (20, 20, 20)$. Here $\mathbf{g}Q = (15, 20, 20)$. Since $\mathbf{g}Q \leq \mathbf{g}$, and we can apply part (iii) of our Theorem to assure us of condition (3), $\mathbf{g}$ is feasible for all $\mathbf{m}$ and $\mathbf{f} = (5, 0, 0)$.

We can also compute $\mathbf{h} = (I - Q)\mathbf{1} = \begin{pmatrix} 0 \\ 0 \\ \frac{1}{4} \end{pmatrix}$, and $\mathbf{gh} = (\frac{1}{4})g_C$. Hence the total amount of money that needs to be supplied per period is $\frac{1}{4}$ of the amount desired for City C. This is intuitively plausible, and can be checked on the two numerical examples.

Let us now suppose that the government has access only to Cities A and B.

$$T = \begin{pmatrix} \frac{1}{2} & \frac{1}{4} \\ \frac{1}{4} & \frac{1}{2} \end{pmatrix} \qquad U = \begin{pmatrix} \frac{1}{4} \\ \frac{1}{4} \end{pmatrix}$$

$$V = (0 \quad \frac{1}{4}) \qquad W = (\frac{1}{2})$$

$$(I - W)^{-1} = (2) \quad U(I - W)^{-1} = \begin{pmatrix} \frac{1}{2} \\ \frac{1}{2} \end{pmatrix} \quad Q^* = \begin{pmatrix} \frac{1}{2} & \frac{3}{8} \\ \frac{1}{4} & \frac{5}{8} \end{pmatrix}$$

We must now require

$$g_C = g_A/2 + g_B/2.$$

Then $f_C = 0$, and $\mathbf{f}^* = \mathbf{g}^*(I - Q^*)$ is

$$f_A = g_A/2 - g_B/4; \quad f_B = 3g_B/8 - 3g_A/8.$$

Thus $f_A + f_B = g_A/8 + g_B/8 = g_C/4$, as was required. We can no longer achieve the goal (12, 8, 20) but (20, 20, 20) is still obtainable.

7. **Historical note.** Potential theory is an important branch of classical physics. Probabilistic generalizations of part of this theory were worked out by J. L. Doob and G. A. Hunt. They showed that a discrete analogue of three-dimensional potential theory exists for three-dimensional random walks, which can be generalized to all transient Markov chains. In this theory the matrix N plays the role of the classical potential operator.

The present authors showed that an analogue of two-dimensional potential theory for two-dimensional random walks can be generalized to all ergodic Markov chains. In this extension the matrix Z plays the role of the potential operator. (Actually, the authors have extended potential theory to a wide class of infinite chains, but in this case the theory becomes more complex than that shown here.) These results, together with a summary of the results of Doob and Hunt as they pertain to Markov chains, may be found in the authors' paper, "Potentials for Denumerable Markov Chains," *Journal of Mathematical Analysis and Applications*.

In either case, it turns out that $\mathbf{f}$ plays the role of the charge and that $\mathbf{g}$ is an analogue of a classical potential. The present chapter illustrates but one of many possible applications of these generalized potential theory concepts.

EXERCISES

Problems 1 through 7 refer to the following example: There are two cities; City A keeps $3/4$ of its currency in each period and sends $1/4$ to City B, and City B keeps $1/2$ and sends $1/2$ to A. At the beginning A has 12 units of currency and B has 4.

1. Find P.

2. Compute $\boldsymbol{\alpha}$. To what does P^n converge?

3. Compute Z.

4. How must $\mathbf{g}$ be chosen so that the currency be equalized in the long run? What choice of $\mathbf{f}$ will accomplish this?

5. Check your answer by means of (4).

6. Compute the distribution of currency after two periods; namely, add $\mathbf{f}$ and then redistribute according to P and add $\mathbf{f}$; then redistribute again and add $\mathbf{f}$. Is there evidence of convergence?

7. Let $\mathbf{f} = (2,2)$. Compute the currency distribution after two periods, as in Exercise 6. Is the distribution converging?

Problems 8 through 11 refer to the following example: There are two cities; A keeps half its currency and ships half to B in each period; B keeps half its currency and ships $1/4$ to A and $1/4$ overseas. At the beginning each city has 10 units of currency.

8. Set up Q and P.

9. Compute $I - Q$ and N.

10. Suppose that the government aims at the goal $\mathbf{g} = (12, 8)$. Find the correct method, and check your answer by computing $\mathbf{f}N$. Check the formula $\mathbf{f1} = \mathbf{gh}$.

11. Is the goal $\mathbf{g} = (10, 56)$ feasible?

Problems 12 through 15 refer to the following example: There are three cities. Currency from Cities A and C is redistributed evenly among the three cities in each period. B keeps half its currency and sends $1/4$ to each of the other cities. At the beginning $\mathbf{m} = (10, 7, 5)$. Currency can be supplied only in Cities A and B.

12. Set up P.

13. Find $U(I - W)^{-1}$ and P^*.

14. It is decided that in the long run A should have 11 units of currency. What will B and C have? Is the goal feasible?

15. Find $\mathbf{f}$ in two ways, by means of (6) and by (9).

16. If the government does not interfere in a conserving system, then the distribution of money approaches a multiple of $\boldsymbol{\alpha}$. Let $\hat{p}_{ij}$ be the fraction of the money in city i that *comes from* city j in the long run. Prove that $\hat{p}_{ij} = \alpha_j p_{ji}/\alpha_i$.

17. Using the result of Exercise 16, show that the ergodic example of Section 6 satisfies the condition of "equal exchange," i.e., that $\hat{p}_{ij} = p_{ij}$.

18. Prove that a nonconserving system cannot be in equilibrium without government aid; i.e. there is no distribution $\mathbf{m}$ such that $\mathbf{m}Q = \mathbf{m}$.

19. Assume that P is regular, $\mathbf{g}$ is positive, and $\mathbf{g}P \leq \mathbf{g}$. Show that

(a) $$\mathbf{g} \geq \mathbf{g}P \geq \mathbf{g}P^2 \geq \cdots \geq 0$$

(b) $$\mathbf{g} = \mathbf{g}P^{n+1} + (\mathbf{g} - \mathbf{g}P)(I + P + P^2 + \cdots + P^n).$$

Using (a) and (b) show that $\mathbf{g} = \mathbf{g}P$.

20. Under the conditions of Section 5, show that if $\mathbf{g}^*Q^* \leq \mathbf{g}^*$, then (3) is satisfied for all n.

21. In the ergodic example in Section 6, under the restriction that the government can step in only in Cities A and B, is $\mathbf{g} = (^{125}\!\!/_9,\ ^1\!\!/_{12},\ ^{253}\!\!/_{36})$ a feasible goal?

22. Give an economic interpretation of the vector $\mathbf{h} = (I - Q)\mathbf{1}$ for a nonconserving system. Use this interpretation to explain why the total amount of money supplied must be $\mathbf{g}\mathbf{h}$.

PROJECT 1

Let us suppose that the central government is in a position to supply money to the various cities, but it cannot remove it from circulation. How does this affect the problem of long-range stability?

Clearly, in a conserving system there is little choice in reaching a stable distribution, since the condition $\mathbf{f}\mathbf{1} = 0$ can be satisfied only if $\mathbf{f} = 0$, i.e., only if the government does not interfere. What happens in this case?

More interesting is the question for a nonconserving system. What new restriction must be imposed on $\mathbf{g}$? Show that the feasible goals for a given total amount of money to be supplied form a convex set which can be described in terms of N.

Suppose that goal $\mathbf{g}$ can be achieved by supplying money only in select cities, and $\mathbf{g}'$ is a feasible goal such that $g_i' \geq g_i$ for all select cities i. Show that $\mathbf{g}' \geq \mathbf{g}$ for all cities. (It is worth verifying that this result is not true if money may be withdrawn by the government.)

PROJECT 2

Consider a different scheme for government action. The government supplies amounts $\mathbf{f}$ to the various cities at the beginning, but in the next period this supply is cut to $r\mathbf{f}$, where $0 < r < 1$, and in period k only $r^k\mathbf{f}$ is supplied. In other words, the government gradually withdraws from interference in the flow of currency.

Develop this model in as much detail as possible.

CHAPTER VII

Branching Processes

1. Statement of problems. In this chapter we shall consider two problems which seem to be quite different. We shall solve one of the problems and show that the solution of this problem leads to a solution of the other problem.

The first problem that we consider is subject to a number of interpretations. One of these is the following: We consider a species of animal that reproduces asexually. Each animal, before dying, produces a certain number of new animals. We start with a single animal and are interested in studying the way in which the population of animals grows. For example, we shall determine whether or not the species eventually dies out. This problem was first studied by Galton late in the last century. Galton was interested in the problem of survival of family names.

The second problem that we consider is in business economics. We consider a business which performs a service for its customers. We assume that customers arrive and wait in line until it is their turn for service. When their turn for service comes, the service takes a certain length of time, after which they depart. An example would be the post office stamp window. In this problem we are interested in the evolution of the line and in the length of time during which the servicer is kept busy.

2. Mathematical formulation of the first problem. The basic assumption in the first problem is that any animal is like any other animal, and that the probability of having a certain number of offspring is the same for each animal in each generation. Hence the process is determined by numbers p_k, where p_k is the probability for any animal of having exactly k offspring. Clearly, $p_k \geq 0$ and $\sum\limits_{k=0}^{\infty} p_k = 1$.

We can treat our problem as a Markov chain with infinitely many states. The state at the mth step represents the total number of animals in the mth generation. Since we assume that we start with one animal, the starting position is 1. The probability of moving from one state to another is easy to describe, but somewhat messy to compute explicitly: If we are in state n, we perform n independent trials, in each of which the outcome k has probability p_k, and our new state is the sum of the outcomes. Thus if we have only one animal, then the next state is k with a probability of p_k. If we have two animals in some generation, i.e., we are in State 2 on some step, then we can have four animals in the next generation in several ways; e.g., the first animal may have four offspring and the second none, or both may have exactly two offspring. Thus the probability p_{24} of moving from State 2 to State 4 in one step is $p_4 p_0 + p_3 p_1 + p_2 p_2 + p_1 p_3 + p_0 p_4$. A Markov chain of the type we are considering is called a *branching process*.

The state 0 is an absorbing state. When the process reaches this state, the species has died out, and so the process remains in position 0 forever. One of the interesting questions is whether the species is sure to die out. (It is important to remember that our chain has an infinite number of states. In a finite absorbing chain, of course, the probability of absorption would always be 1.) We let d stand for the probability that the species eventually dies out. We let d_m stand for the probability that the species has died out by step m (i.e., by the mth generation). Thus $d = \lim_{m \to \infty} d_m$. We will also be interested in the probability s_n that there will be exactly n animals in the family before the family dies out. If the family does die out, it has only a finite number of animals in it; otherwise it has infinitely many, and hence $d = \Sigma s_n$.

We shall have occasion to refer to the mean $M = \Sigma k \cdot p_k$ of the number of offspring of a given animal, and to the mean number of animals in the entire family, $N = \Sigma n \cdot s_n$.

We shall illustrate our results in terms of *geometric distributions*, i.e., the case in which $p_k = (1 - a)a^k$, $k = 0, 1, 2, \ldots$ for some number $0 < a < 1$. We can verify that $\Sigma p_k = 1$ by summing a geometric series. The mean is $M = (1 - a)\Sigma k \cdot a^k = a/(1 - a)$.

3. Solution of the first problem. We have not given an explicit formula for p_{ij}, the transition probabilities. However, we shall find that we can compute the quantities d, d_m, s_n, and N by other methods. The principal tool will be the generating function $f(t) = \sum_{k=0}^{\infty} p_k t^k$. (See Appendix D.) This is well defined for at least $0 \leq t \leq 1$, and $f(1) = \Sigma p_k = 1$, whereas $f'(1) = \Sigma p_k \cdot k = M$. We also know that f' and f'' are nonnegative in this interval; hence, the graph of $y = f(t)$ has the general appearance of the curve shown in Figure 19.

We shall be interested in the intersection of this curve with the straight line $y = ct$, for certain constants $c \geq 1$. That is, we wish to solve

(1) $f(t) = ct$ for $c \geq 1$, $0 \leq t \leq 1$.

From the fact that $y = f(t)$ is convex ($f''(t) \geq 0$), we see that there are at most two intersections. Since $f(0) = p_0 \geq 0 = c \cdot 0$, and as $f(1) = 1 \leq c \cdot 1$, there must be at least one solution in the interval. In case there are two

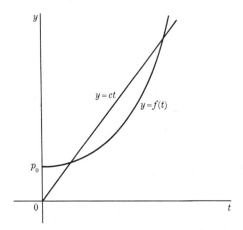

Figure 19

solutions in the interval $0 \leq t \leq 1$, we shall be interested in the smaller root. From Figure 19 we see that this root is characterized by the fact that the slope of the curve is less than the slope of the line. Hence to obtain the smaller root of (1) we must require

$$(2) \qquad\qquad f'(t) \leq c.$$

Equality occurs if there is tangency, i.e., if there is a single intersection point.

EXAMPLE. In the case of a geometric distribution, $f(t) = (1 - a)\Sigma(at)^k = (1 - a)/(1 - at)$, and $f'(t) = a(1 - a)/(1 - at)^2$. Hence $M = f'(1) = a/(1 - a)$, as noted before. After simplification Equation (1) takes on the form $act^2 - ct + 1 - a = 0$. If $c > 1$, there are two real roots; one between 0 and 1, and the other above 1. If $c = 1$, the roots are $(1 - a)/a$ and 1.

We shall now proceed to find formulas for our various quantities, starting with the probability d_m that the species dies out by the mth generation. We shall compute these values recursively, i.e., obtain an answer for d_{m+1} in terms of d_m.

Since we start with one individual, d_0 is 0. The family dies out in the first generation if and only if this original animal has no offspring. Hence, $d_1 = p_0$. Now let us suppose that d_m is known for some m, and let us compute d_{m+1}. In the first generation there were k offspring. Each of these may be thought of as the heads of a new family. If the original family dies out by the $(m+1)$st generation, that means that each of the offspring families dies out by the mth generation. Since the probability that any one family dies out by the mth generation is d_m, and since the k new families reproduce independently of each other, the probability that they all die out is $d_m{}^k$. Of course, we do not know the exact value of k, but we do know that a value k has probability p_k. Hence the probability of dying out in $m + 1$ generations is given by

$$(3) \qquad d_{m+1} = \sum_{k=0}^{\infty} p_k \cdot d_m{}^k = f(d_m).$$

For example, $d_1 = f(d_0) = f(0) = p_0$, as noted before. This provides a step-by-step method of computing the probabilities d_m. The procedure is illustrated in Figure 20.

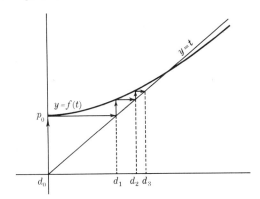

Figure 20

Next we turn to the probability that the species dies out, $d = \lim_{m \to \infty} d_m$. By passing to the limit on both sides of Equation (3) we find that

$$(4) \qquad d = f(d).$$

(We could also have found this relationship by a direct probability argument.) The values d_m are clearly monotone increasing, and they start with 0. Hence we see from Figure 20 that they can never get past the first intersection of the curve and the line. But (4) states that d is a root of (1) with $c = 1$, and hence is an intersection point. Thus d must be the smallest root of (1).

We are thus directed to find the smallest root of Equation (1), with $c = 1$. Since $f(1) = 1$, $t = 1$ is a root in this case. Is it the smaller root? For this we must test Equation (2): $t = 1$ is the smaller root if and only if $M = f'(1) \leq 1$. In this case $d = 1$, otherwise $d < 1$. Thus if the mean number of offspring for a given animal is 1 or less, then the family is sure to die out. But if the mean M is greater than 1, then it has a chance of surviving forever; hence, d is less than 1. We can find this value of d by finding the smaller root of (4).

EXAMPLE CONTINUED. For the geometric distributions, Equation (4) takes on the form $ad^2 - d + 1 - a = 0$, and the two roots are 1 and $(1 - a)/a = 1/M$. Thus, if $M \leq 1$, then 1 is the smallest root, and hence $d = 1$. But if $M > 1$, then $d = 1/M$ is the smaller root, and so in this case the probability of dying out is inversely proportional to the mean number of offspring per animal.

Let us next consider the probability s_n that there are exactly n animals in the family before it dies out. As we noted before, $d = \Sigma s_n$ for any branching process.

We introduce an order among the animals in the family. First will be the original ancestor. Then we order the descendants of the first generation, then those of the second, etc., according to any convenient rule (say by "age"). Let ν_k be the number of animals that had k offspring. If there were exactly n animals, then

$$(5) \qquad \Sigma \nu_k = n \quad \text{and} \quad \Sigma k \nu_k = n - 1.$$

The former expresses the fact that there were n potential ancestors, and the latter expresses the fact that there were $n - 1$ descendants. Naturally $\nu_k = 0$ if $k > n$. Let $\alpha(n; \nu_0, \ldots, \nu_n)$ be the number of possible histories for the family in which a total of n animals exists such that ν_k of them have k descendants. Of course, $\alpha = 0$ unless (5) is satisfied. We then have

$$(6) \qquad s_n = \Sigma \alpha(n; \nu_0, \ldots, \nu_n) p_0{}^{\nu_0} p_1{}^{\nu_1} \cdots p_n{}^{\nu_n},$$

where the sum is taken over all possible combinations of ν_k. Making use of the Lemma in Appendix E, we obtain

$$(7) \qquad s_n = \frac{1}{n} \sum \binom{n}{\nu_0, \nu_1, \ldots, \nu_n} p_0{}^{\nu_0} p_1{}^{\nu_1} \cdots p_n{}^{\nu_n}.$$

Although Formula (7) provides a method for computing s_n, it is not a very practical method. We can find a simpler procedure by introducing the generating function $g(u) = \Sigma s_k \cdot u^k$. We will show that this generating function can be computed from f.

The connection is most simply established by means of a trick. We introduce a modified branching process by letting $p_k{}^* = p_k x^k / f(x)$, for a certain real number x whose value will be chosen later. We can compute our various quantities for the modified process. In particular, in the computation of $s_n{}^*$ from (7) we note that the terms differ from those of s_n by a factor which, because of (5), always simplifies to $x^{n-1}/f(x)^n$. Hence,

$$(8) \qquad g^*(u) = \sum_{n=1}^{\infty} [x^{n-1} s_n / f(x)^n] u^n = (1/x) g(xu/f(x)).$$

Or, solving for g, $g(u) = x g^*(uf(x)/x)$. This holds for every x, and so we can select as our x the smallest root of the following equation.

(9) $uf(x) = x$ such that $0 \leq x \leq 1$.

This is a special case of (1) with $c = 1/u$, and we know that there is a root—at least as long as $0 \leq u \leq 1$. From (2) we find that $f'(x) \leq 1/u$ for the smallest root, which by (9) is equivalent to $xf'(x) \leq f(x)$.

A simple computation shows that the mean number of offspring in the modified process is $M^* = xf'(x)/f(x)$, which we now know to be at most 1. But then the modified process necessarily dies out, and $d^* = 1$, by our previous result. However, $1 = d^* = \Sigma s_n{}^* = g^*(1) = (1/x)g(x/f(x)) = (1/x)g(u)$ for u as in (9). Thus the smallest root x of (9) is equal to $g(u)$.

Our trick has thus yielded a method for computing the generating function g: For any u such that $0 \leq u \leq 1$, $x = g(u)$ is the smallest root of (9). If this function is expanded in a power series, the coefficients are s_n. In particular, $d = g(1)$ is the smallest root of $f(x) = x$, which yields a second proof for a previous result.

Finally we shall compute the mean number of animals in the entire family, $N = \Sigma s_n \cdot n$. The total number of animals may be computed by counting the original animal, and adding the total number of animals in the families of all the first generation offspring. But since each offspring is like the original animal, the mean number of animals in its family must be N; hence, if there are k offspring in the first generation, the mean total number of animals (not counting the original one) is kN. Thus, if N is finite, then

$$N = 1 + \Sigma p_k \cdot kN = 1 + MN$$

or

$$N = 1/(1 - M).$$

This shows that N is finite only if $M < 1$. Thus we have three distinct cases for our quantities:

  Case I. $M < 1$, $d = 1$, $N = 1/(1 - M)$.
  Case II. $M = 1$, $d = 1$, N infinite.
  Case III. $M > 1$, $d < 1$ is smaller root of (4), N infinite.

And, in any case, we find d_m recursively from (3), and we find $g(u)$ for each u as the smallest root of (9)—which yields s_n from its Taylor expansion.

EXAMPLE CONTINUED. For our geometric distributions, (9) takes the form $ax^2 - x + u(1 - a) = 0$, and the smaller root is

$$g(u) = \frac{1 - \sqrt{1 - 4au(1 - a)}}{2a}.$$

If we expand this in a Taylor series, we find that the coefficients are

$$s_n = (1/an)[a(1 - a)]^n \binom{2n - 2}{n - 1}.$$

Let us check this result by computing it directly from (6). In the geometric case $p_0{}^{\nu_0} \cdots p_n{}^{\nu_n} = (1 - a)^n a^{n-1}$ always, by (5). Therefore,

$$s_n = (1/a)[a(1 - a)]^n \Sigma \alpha(n; \nu_0, \ldots, \nu_n).$$

But this latter sum is $(1/n) \begin{pmatrix} 2n - 2 \\ n - 1 \end{pmatrix}$ by the Lemma in Appendix E.

Since $M = a/(1 - a)$, we have the following three cases for the geometric distributions:

Case I. $a < \frac{1}{2}$, $d = 1$, $N = (1 - a)/(1 - 2a)$.
Case II. $a = \frac{1}{2}$, $d = 1$, N infinite.
Case III. $a > \frac{1}{2}$, $d = (1 - a)/a = 1/M$, N infinite.

4. Mathematical formulation of the second problem. We wish to make a simple mathematical model which will describe the way that customers arrive and are serviced. We assume that there is only one server. We shall measure time in some conveniently small unit. We assume that in each unit of time there is a fixed probability a that a customer arrives, and hence a probability $1 - a$ that no customer arrives, and that the time unit is small enough so that at most one customer arrives in any one time unit.

We assume that for each customer there is a probability p_j that his service time is j units long. We consider in detail two different choices for these service time probabilities. The first is called the *geometric service time*. This is obtained by assuming that there is a probability s that a customer finishes his service in any one time unit of service. Then $p_j = (1 - s)^{j-1} s$ for $j = 1, 2, \ldots$. The second type of service that we shall consider is the *constant service time*. For this we assume that each customer requires a fixed number c of time units for his service.

We make the convention that the customer arrives at the beginning of a time unit and is served immediately if no other person is being served. If someone else is being served when he arrives, he joins the line waiting to be served. We shall define a *busy period* to be the period of time between the arrival of the first customer and the first time after this that the server finishes his task (i.e., he finishes serving a customer, and there are none in line). We are interested first in finding conditions under which the busy periods will end (i.e., the line will not grow indefinitely), second in finding the distribution of the number of customers served in a busy period, and third in finding the mean total length of a busy period.

5. Solution of the second problem. We shall consider first the problem of the number of customers in a busy period. We shall solve this problem by forming a branching process which we shall call the *customer branching process*. For any customer we define the "offspring" of this customer to be all the customers that arrive during his service time. For each of the customers the number of offspring can be thought of as the sum of a random number of independent functions—the functions giving the number of people (0 or 1) that arrive in a particular time interval of his service and the random number being the length of his service period. In general, if $h(t)$ is the generating function for the number of arrivals in one time unit, and $k(t)$ is the generating function for the number of time units of service, the generating function $f(t)$ for the number of offspring of a customer is $k(h(t))$. (See Appendix D.) In our example this will be the same for all customers in a busy period except for its first customer. No one can arrive during the first customer's first unit of service since he himself arrives during this time period; hence, the distribution for his offspring will differ from that of the others. Therefore, we shall start considering the branching process after the first person has been served, and the initial state will consist of the number of people who arrive while the first person is being served.

Putting all of this together we see that the total number of customers during a busy period can be considered to be a branching process with a distribution of offspring determined by the above generating function $f(t) = k(h(t))$, but with a random initial state, i.e., the number of customers that arrive while the first person is being served. We can now use the results of the first problem to find the total number of customers during a busy period. We note first that from our solution to the first problem, the branching process will die out (i.e., the busy period will end) with probability 1 if and only if the mean M of the distribution of offspring is ≤ 1. But this is

$$M = f'(1) = k'(h(1)) \cdot h'(1) = k'(1) \cdot h'(1).$$

Thus, the mean number of offspring of a customer is the product of the mean number of arrivals in a unit time and the mean service time, and the busy period is sure to end if this product is at most 1.

The generating function for the number of arrivals in a unit time interval is always

(10)
$$h(t) = 1 - a + at,$$

since with probability $1 - a$ no one arrives and otherwise one person arrives.

We illustrate the calculation of the distribution of the number of customers in a busy period for the case of constant service time $c = 2$, i.e., when each customer is served in exactly 2 time units. The generating function for the service time is

$$k(t) = t^2.$$

Hence the generating function for the number of offspring of a customer after the first is

$$f(t) = k(h(t)) = (1 - a + at)^2.$$

Thus, to find the generating function for the total number of offspring produced by a customer after the first one we must solve (9) or

$$u(1 - a + at)^2 = t.$$

Solving this equation and taking the minimum solution we obtain the generating function

(11) $$g(u) = \frac{1 - 2ua(1 - a) - \sqrt{1 - 4ua(1 - a)}}{2a^2u}$$

for the total number of offspring.

The generating function for the number of offspring of the first customer is

(12) $$f_1(t) = 1 - a + at,$$

since he has an offspring if and only if a customer arrives in the second time unit of his service.

Thus, the total number of customers served during a busy period has generating function

(13) $$q(u) = u \cdot f_1(g(u)) = \frac{1 - \sqrt{1 - 4ua(1 - a)}}{2a}.$$

(We multiplied by u so that the initial customer would be counted.) This is the same generating function that we obtained for our geometric example in the first problem. Hence, if s_n denotes the probability that exactly n customers are served in a busy period for constant service time $c = 2$,

(14) $$s_n = (1/an)[a(1 - a)]^n \binom{2n - 2}{n - 1}.$$

A similar procedure may be carried out for geometric service time, but the formulas are more complicated When this is done, the generating function for the total number of customers served in a busy period is found to be

(15) $$q(u) = \frac{s}{2}u + \frac{B}{2a}(1 - \sqrt{1 - Cu + Du^2})$$

where $B = 1 - (1 - a)(1 - s)$, $C = 2sa[1 + (1 - s)(1 - a)]/B^2$,   and $D = (as/B)^2$.

It is interesting to compare the geometric service time with the constant service time when the arrivals are the same and the mean service times are the same.

The mean time for a constant service time c is, of course, c. For a geometric service time the mean is

$$\sum_{j=1}^{\infty} j(1 - s)^{j-1}s = 1/s.$$

Hence we choose $s = 1/c$.

We do this for the case $a = .3$, and a geometric distribution with $s = \frac{1}{2}$, and constant service time $c = 2$. The values for s_n for these two cases are given in Table 1.

n	GEOMETRIC SERVICE TIME $s = \frac{1}{2}$ $a = .3$	CONSTANT SERVICE TIME $c = 2$ $a = .3$
1	.770	.700
2	.096	.146
3	.046	.062
4	.026	.032
5	.016	.019
>5	.046	.040

Table 1   Table of s_n

As would be expected, we see that extreme cases are more probable in the geometric distribution than in the constant service distribution: For the geometric case it is more likely that only one person is served or that more than five are served in a busy period.

This example was carried out by having a machine generate the customers and the service times. The machine carried out a thousand time units and obtained 174 busy periods for the geometric distribution and 170 busy periods for the constant service time. The number of observed periods with a given number of customers and the number predicted from the above distributions is shown in Table 2. A simple statistical test shows that in each case observations and predictions are in good agreement.

We show next that a similar technique enables us to find the distribution of the total number of time units in a busy period. For this we define a new branching process which we call the *time branching process*.† We define the "offspring" of a time unit to be the time units of service for the customers which arrive in this time unit. The number of offspring is the sum of a random number of independent functions, where the functions are the service times, and the random number the number of arrivals. Hence the basic generating function for this branching process is $h(k(t))$ where h and

† The suggestion of using the customer process is due to D. G. Kendall, and the time branching process to I. J. Good.

Number of busy periods in which exactly n customers are served
(Results of 1000 time units of machine generated service)

n	GEOMETRIC SERVICE TIME 174 BUSY PERIODS $a = .3, \quad s = \frac{1}{2}$		CONSTANT SERVICE TIME 170 BUSY PERIODS $a = .3, \quad c = 2$	
	OBSERVED	PREDICTED	OBSERVED	PREDICTED
1	131	134.0	122	119.0
2	17	16.7	26	24.8
3	11	8.0	8	10.5
4	7	4.5	6	5.4
5	2	2.8	3	3.2
>5	6	8.0	5	6.8

Table 2

k are, as before, the generating functions for the number of arrivals in a
unit of time and the service time of a customer. As in the customer branching process, we must consider the first unit of time separately. We take the
first customer's service time as the random initial state for the branching
process.

For the constant service time the total time in a busy period is simply a
multiple of the number of customers served, and hence it is of no new interest.
Thus we shall consider only the geometric case.

The generating function for the service time is

$$k(t) = \sum_{j=1}^{\infty} (1 - s)^{j-1} st^j = \frac{st}{1 - (1 - s)t}.$$

The generating function for the number of arrivals in a unit of time is as
in (10). Hence the generating function for the number of offspring in our
time branching process is

$$\bar{f}(t) = h(k(t)) = 1 - a + \frac{ast}{1 - (1 - s)t}.$$

To find the total time generating function we must solve (9), or

(16) $u\bar{f}(t) = t.$

As for the customer process, the general case is somewhat complicated, so we shall consider only a special case. Let us select the case $a = s = \frac{1}{2}$. This is interesting, because the mean number of offspring is 1, so that the mean duration of the busy period will be infinite. For this case we must solve the equation

$$u\left(\frac{1}{2-t}\right) = t.$$

Carrying this out, we obtain the generating function

(17) $$\bar{g}(u) = 1 - \sqrt{1-u}$$

for the total number of time units generated by a unit time interval in the branching process. We must next take into account the fact that we have a random starting state. The probability that the initial state is j is $(\frac{1}{2})^{j+1}$, $j = 0, 1, 2, \ldots.$ The generating function for this state is

(18) $$\bar{f}_1(t) = \frac{1}{2-t}.$$

Thus, the generating function for the total number of time units of the busy period is

(19) $$\bar{q}(u) = u\bar{f}_1(\bar{g}(u)) = 1 - \sqrt{1-u}.$$

We note that by chance this agrees with (17).

Hence if $\bar{s}_n$ is the probability of exactly n time units in the busy period, we have

(20) $$\bar{s}_n = (-1)^{n+1}\binom{\frac{1}{2}}{n} = \frac{1}{n}\binom{2n-2}{n-1}2^{-2n+1}.$$

In Table 3 we give the results of a machine experiment comparing these with the expected values. It will be noted that, although there were very large busy periods, it is still true that a period of length 1 is the most probable single value.

Finally, let us compute L, the mean length of a busy period. For the case of constant service time of 2, the mean number of customers per busy period is $q'(1) = (1-a)/(1-2a)$, and hence $L = 2(1-a)/(1-2a)$.

This special trick works only for the constant case. In general, we have $\bar{q}(u) = u \cdot \bar{f}_1(\bar{g}(u))$, and hence

$$\bar{q}'(u) = \bar{f}_1(\bar{g}(u)) + u \cdot \bar{f}_1'(\bar{g}(u)) \cdot \bar{g}'(u)$$

and $$L = \bar{q}'(1) = 1 + \bar{f}_1'(1)\bar{g}'(1).$$

Number of busy periods of length n
(Results of 1000 time units of machine
generated service)
$a = s = \frac{1}{2}$

n	96 OBSERVED BUSY PERIODS	EXPECTED $96 \times \mathfrak{z}_n$
1	46	48
2	11	12
3	7	6
4–6	10	8.34
7–10	3	4.74
11–20	5	4.87
21–50	9	4.38
>50	5	7.67

Table 3

If we let $\bar{M} = \bar{f}'(1)$, $\bar{M}_1 = \bar{f}_1'(1)$, and $\bar{N} = \bar{g}'(1)$, in analogy to the first problem, then $\bar{N} = 1/(1 - \bar{M})$. Hence

(21) $$L = 1 + \bar{M}_1/(1 - \bar{M}).$$

In particular, for the geometric case $\bar{f}(t) = 1 - a + \dfrac{ast}{1 - (1 - s)t}$ and $\bar{f}_1(t) = \dfrac{s}{1 - (1 - s)t}$. Hence $\bar{M} = a/s$ and $\bar{M}_1 = (1 - s)/s$. Substituting into (21) we obtain $L = (1 - a)/(s - a)$. For $s = \frac{1}{2}$ this agrees with the value of L obtained for the constant case above. For example, if $a = .3$, then $L = \frac{7}{2}$ for either the geometric case with $s = \frac{1}{2}$ or for the constant case $c = 2$.

The process divides into slack periods and busy periods, which alternate. The mean length of slack periods is $\dfrac{1 - a}{a}$. Let us call a slack period followed by a busy period a *cycle*. The mean length of a cycle in the geometric case is $\dfrac{1 - a}{a} + \dfrac{1 - a}{s - a} = \dfrac{s(1 - a)}{a(s - a)}$. If $a = .3$, $s = \frac{1}{2}$, this is $\frac{35}{6}$.

And the length of a cycle in the constant case $c = 2$ is the same. Thus in 1000 periods we can expect about $1000 \times \frac{6}{35} = 171.4$ cycles, and the same number of busy periods. We observed 174 in one example, 170 in the other, in excellent agreement.

EXERCISES

1. In the first problem let $p_k = 2^k/3^{k+1}$. Find $f(t)$, M, N, and d, and interpret your results.

2. In the first problem, let us assume that each animal has either one offspring or two, and the two possibilities are equally likely. Discuss this case completely.

3. In the first problem, let us assume that half the animals do not reproduce, whereas the remaining ones are equally likely to have one or two offspring. Discuss this case completely. In particular, find s_1, s_2, and s_3 from $g(u)$. Check these values by a direct computation.

4. In the second problem, let us assume that the probability of a customer arriving in a given period is $\frac{1}{2}$. Find the probability that the total number of customers served in a busy period is 1, 2, and 3, assuming

   (a) Each customer takes 2 periods to be served.

   (b) The service time is geometric, with mean 2.

5. Let us suppose that in the reproduction of species of animals the distribution of offspring alternates from generation to generation between a distribution whose generating function is f and one whose generating function is $\bar{f}$. If the probability that the species dies out is d if we start with an f generation, and $\bar{d}$ if we start with an $\bar{f}$ generation, find d and $\bar{d}$ in a manner analogous to the way d was found in Section 3.

6. In Exercise 5, let N and $\bar{N}$ be the mean number of animals in the entire history of the family, depending on whether we start with an f or $\bar{f}$ generation. Prove that N is finite if and only if $\bar{N}$ is finite, and find a formula for both in the finite case.

7. In Exercises 5 and 6, suppose that the odd-numbered generations have one or two offspring (with equal probability), and that in the even-numbered generations there is probability $\frac{3}{4}$ for one offspring and $\frac{1}{4}$ for no offspring. Find d, $\bar{d}$, N, and $\bar{N}$.

8. Modify Exercise 7 by assuming that in the even-numbered generations there is an even chance of one or no offspring. Find d, $\bar{d}$, N, and $\bar{N}$.

9. Let $f(s)$ be the generating function for the number of particles produced by a single particle in a branching process. Let $f^{(n)}(s)$ be the generating function for the number of particles in the nth generation. Show that $f^{(n)}(s) = f(f^{(n-1)}(s))$. (*Hint:* Use Theorem 1 in Appendix D.) Using this result, show how to obtain $f^{(n)}(s)$ from $f(s)$.

10. Using the result of Exercise 9, show that if M is the mean number of particles produced by a single particle, the mean number of particles in the nth generation is M^n.

Exercises 11 through 14 apply to a branching process in which j particles are produced by a single particle with probability $\frac{1}{2}^{j+1}$.

11. Show that the generating function for the number of particles in the nth generation is $f^{(n)}(s) = \dfrac{n - (n-1)s}{(n+1) - ns}$.

12. Using the result of Exercise 11, show that the probability that the nth generation consists of j particles is

$$p_j^{(n)} = \begin{cases} \dfrac{1}{n(n+1)} \left(\dfrac{n}{n+1}\right)^j & \text{if } j \geq 1 \\[2ex] \dfrac{n}{n+1} & \text{if } j = 0. \end{cases}$$

13. Show that the probability that the process dies out exactly at the nth generation is $1/[n(n+1)]$. Prove that the sum of these is 1.

14. Show that the mean lifetime is infinite, even though $d = 1$.

15. Consider the time branching process for the case of geometric service time with $a = s = \frac{1}{2}$. Using the fact that the generating function for the length of a busy period was found to be $1 - (1 - u)^{\frac{1}{2}}$, show that the tail generating function for the number of customers served is $h(u) = (1 - u)^{-\frac{1}{2}}$. (See Appendix D.) Using this, show that the probability that a busy period has more than n time units is

$$q_n = \frac{1}{4^n}\binom{2n}{n}.$$

16. Consider a branching process in which the mean number of particles produced by a single particle is less than one. Let M and V be the mean and variance for the number of particles produced by a single particle, and N, $\overline{V}$ the mean and variance for the total number of particles produced by the process. Let $f(s)$ and $g(s)$ be the generating functions for the number produced by a single particle and the total number, respectively. Using the fact that

$$sf(g(s)) = g(s),$$

and using the method of obtaining means and variances from the generating functions (see Appendix D), give a new derivation of the fact that

$$N = \frac{1}{1 - M},$$

and show that

$$\overline{V} = \frac{V}{(1 - M)^3}.$$

17. The generating function for the total number of customers served in a busy period is $q(u) = u \cdot f_1(g(u))$. If M and V are the mean and variance of the basic generating function f, and M_1 and V_1 of f_1, show that

(a) The mean number of customers served in a busy period will be $1 + M_1/(1 - M)$.

(b) The variance of the number of customers served will be

$$\frac{V_1(1 - M) + M_1 V}{(1 - M)^3}.$$

18. Use the results of Exercise 17 to compute the mean and variance for the number of customers served in a busy period for constant service time $c = 2$, and geometric service time with $s = \frac{1}{2}$. Show that the mean is $\dfrac{1 - a}{1 - 2a}$ in both cases, whereas the variance is $\dfrac{a(1 - a)}{(1 - 2a)^3}$ for the $c = 2$ case and $\dfrac{a(1 - a)(1 + 2a)}{(1 - 2a)^3}$ for the $s = \frac{1}{2}$ case.

19. Carry out the analogues of Exercises 17 and 18 for the generating function $\bar{q}(u)$ of the length of the busy period.

20. Calculate s_n directly from (7) for

(a) $p_0 = p_1 = \frac{1}{2}$.   (Answer: $s_n = \frac{1}{2}^n$.)

(b) $p_0 = p_1 = p_2 = \frac{1}{3}$.

$$\left(\text{Answer: } s_n = \frac{1}{n \cdot 3^n} \sum_{k=1}^{\left[\frac{n+1}{2}\right]} \binom{n}{k,\, n - 2k + 1,\, k - 1}.\right)$$

PROJECT 1

Let us suppose that one half of the customers are served in one period, one half in two periods. Carry out as many of the computations of Section 5 as possible for this case and compare it with the geometric case, where $s = \frac{2}{3}$.

PROJECT 2

In a certain society there are two classes of people, one labeled "upper class" and the other labeled "lower class." Each person in the upper class has j sons with probability r_j. The mean number of sons he has is M_u. Each person in the lower class has j sons with probability s_j. The mean number of sons he has is M_l. Each of these sons become members of either the upper or lower class. Let p_{ij} be the probability that the son of a member of class i becomes a member of class j ($i, j = u$ or l).

Consider first the following deterministic model. We start with $x_u^{(0)}$ individuals in the upper class and $x_l^{(0)}$ in the lower class. These may be represented by the vector $(x_u^{(0)}, x_l^{(0)})$. These individuals will produce $(M_u x_u^{(0)}, M_l x_l^{(0)})$ individuals for the next generation. The next generation then has $(x_u^{(1)}, x_l^{(1)})$ individuals in classes where

$$(x_u^{(1)}, x_l^{(1)}) = (M_u x_u^{(0)}, M_l x_l^{(0)}) \begin{pmatrix} p_{uu} & p_{ul} \\ p_{lu} & p_{ll} \end{pmatrix}.$$

Try to find conditions under which one or both of the classes would disappear, and determine what would happen if they did not. Then consider the branching process model, starting with a single upperclass individual who produces offspring with the given probabilities, and whose offspring move to the two classes with the specified probabilities.

REFERENCES

Feller, W. *An Introduction to Probability Theory and Its Applications*, Vol. 1, 2nd ed. New York: John Wiley and Sons, 1957.

Harris, T. E. "Some Mathematical Models for Branching Processes." *Proc. Second Berkeley Symposium on Mathematical Statistics and Probability*, 1951, pp. 305–328.

Kendall, D. G. "Some Problems in the Theory of Queues." *Journal Royal Statistical Society*, Series B, Vol. 3 (1952), pp. 151–185.

CHAPTER VIII

Organization Theory

Applications of Graph Theory

1. Statement of the problems. Organization theory deals with the way in which large groups of human beings working together are structured. We shall consider three problems in the general area of this theory. The problems are selected because they yield to similar mathematical treatment.

FIRST PROBLEM. We shall consider only a single relationship among the members of the social structure. Do the members have favorable relations, unfavorable, or neutral? By a favorable relationship between two members we shall mean that they like each other, or have similar views, or are able to work together. By an unfavorable relationship we shall mean that they definitely dislike each other, or have opposing views, or naturally oppose each other in their work. Whenever the relationship between two men is not of either of these types, we shall describe it as neutral.

The problem is to give criteria under which the social structure is "balanced" in some reasonable sense of this word. For example, if our social structure is a lawmaking body, we would take as a favorable relationship one in which two members are generally on the same side of major issues. We would like balance to be so defined that it captures our intuition that the U.S. Congress is balanced, and the French Parliament is not.

A second question one might ask about the political structure is whether it is compatible with a two-party system. This would mean that we can divide the legislators into two mutually exclusive classes, so that favorable relations occur only within a class, and unfavorable relations occur only between members of opposite camps. (Naturally, this question is quite different from the historical question of whether the legislators happened to organize into two parties.) Somehow one feels that a two-party system is better balanced than other structures.

SECOND PROBLEM. Next we shall study the communication network of the social structure. Our basic relationship will be "x can send a message (directly) to y." We shall take this in a sense in which it may be possible for x to send a message to y and yet it may be impossible for y to send a message to x, at least directly. It will, however, be natural to assume that any person can send a message to any other person in the system by some circuitous route. Also, we shall assume that a person does not send messages to himself.

For example, the structure may be the New York City Police Department. Any policeman in a radio car can send a message to the central dispatcher and the dispatcher can send a message to him. However, although a cop-on-the-beat can phone in a message to the sergeant-at-the-desk, the sergeant-at-the-desk cannot send a message directly to him. He could, however, ask the dispatcher to call a radio car and ask the policeman in the radio car to give the message to the cop-on-the-beat.

We shall be interested in developing a measure of how important a given person is in the communication network of the structure. We would certainly expect that in any reasonable measure the central dispatcher will be most important. What we would like to measure is how much of the burden falls on a given person in a typical day or typical year of communication.

THIRD PROBLEM. Finally we shall consider the superior-subordinate relation in a hierarchy. We shall be interested in developing a measure of the status of an official in the hierarchy (e.g., an executive in a business firm). Intuitively we feel that the more subordinates a person has, or the higher he is above these subordinates, the greater his status is in the organization. But we would like a numerical measure of his status.

All three of these problems have an interesting common feature: The problems can only be stated vaguely at this stage. We must give a mathematical formulation to the basic relations before we can even ask a precise question. Although this is typical of many problems in the social sciences, our present problems are outstanding examples of this phenomenon.

2. The mathematical tools. We shall find that Graph Theory is a branch of mathematics ideally suited for the precise formulation of our social structures. We shall therefore give a brief introduction to this interesting subject in abstract mathematics.

A *graph* is a finite collection of objects of any sort, which will be called *points*, and of connections between some of the points, called *lines*. We shall denote the points by small letters, and (p,q) will denote the line connecting the point p to the point q. For an ordinary graph a line is determined by the two points; thus (p,q) is the same as (q,p). When we wish to distinguish these lines, we speak of a *directed graph*.

If there is a line (p,q) in the graph, we say that p and q are *adjacent* points. A *path* between points p and q is a sequence of lines of the form (p,a), (a,b), $\ldots$, (c,d), (d,q), where the points a, b, $\ldots$, c, d are all distinct and different from p and q. If $p = q$, then the path is called a *cycle*. A graph is *connected* if there is a path between any two points.

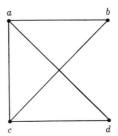

Figure 21 A graph

In Figure 21 we give a graph which has four points and five lines. In this graph (b,a), (a,c), (c,d) is a path from b to d. An example of a cycle is (a,d), (d,c), (c,a). The graph of Figure 21 is connected. As can be seen from this figure, a "line" is usually conveniently represented by a line segment. However, a line in Graph Theory is an abstract object, and it must not be confused with a picture. Thus, the lines (a,d) and (b,c) in Figure 21 have no common point.

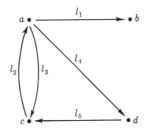

Figure 22 A directed graph

An example of a directed graph is given in Figure 22.

We indicate by arrows the directions of our lines. Thus the directed graph in Figure 22 has the lines (a,b), (a,c), (c,a), (a,d), (d,c). We had to indicate the directed lines (a,c) and (c,a) separately; note, therefore, that (d,a) is not a line in Figure 22. Thus there is a path from d to each of the other points, but there is no path from b to d.

A third type of graph is the signed graph. A *signed graph* is an ordinary graph in which the lines have been labeled either positive or negative. An example of a signed graph is shown in Figure 23.

By a path or a cycle of a signed graph we shall mean a path or cycle of the ordinary graph obtained when the signs of the lines are ignored. We shall say that a path is *positive* if it has an even number of negative signs. It is *negative* if it has an odd number.

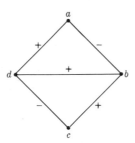

Figure 23   A signed graph

Two graphs G and G' are said to be *isomorphic* if there is a one-to-one correspondence between the points of G and the points of G' which preserves adjacency. That is, G and G' are isomorphic if it is possible to label the points of G by $a, b, c, \ldots, r$ and those of G' by $a', b', c', \ldots, r'$ in such a way that the line (p,q) is on G if and only if the line (p',q') is on G'. The graphs G and G' in Figure 24 are isomorphic.

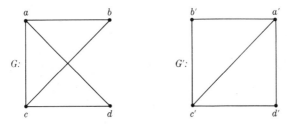

Figure 24   Two isomorphic graphs

Graph Theory studies only those properties of a graph which are invariant under isomorphisms; that is, properties which hold for a graph G if and only if they hold for all graphs isomorphic to G.

By an isomorphism of a signed graph we shall mean a one-to-one transformation which preserves adjacency and the sign of the lines. For a directed graph we shall require that an isomorphism preserve both adjacency and the direction of the connecting lines.

3. Mathematical treatment of the first problem. Signed graphs offer an obvious way of formulating favorable and unfavorable relationships. The members of the social structure are represented by points. A favorable relationship is represented by a line with a + label, and an unfavorable one by a line with a − label. If there is no line between two points, then the relation between the two men is neutral.

The concept of *balance* was introduced by the psychologist Heider to allow him to predict circumstances under which tensions would arise in the structure. "Balance" was to represent the absence of tensions. A simplified version of Heider's ideas may be presented in terms of examples, as follows.

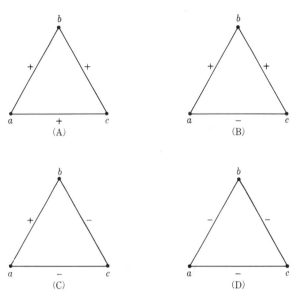

Figure 25

We begin with some decisions in simple cases. In Figure 25 we show all possible signed graphs for three people, if no person is neutral to any other person. (Recall that isomorphic graphs are not to be distinguished from one another.)

In (A) everyone likes everyone else, and we say that this is a balanced situation. In (B), a and b like each other, but are faced with the conflicting situation that one of them likes c and the other does not. Hence we say that this is an unbalanced situation. In (C), a and b like each other and jointly dislike c, and hence we say that this situation is balanced. Finally, in (D), a and b jointly dislike c but are prevented from forming a coalition because of their dislike for each other. Thus we say that this is an unbalanced situation.

If we examine the four cases above, we observe that each graph consists of a single cycle, and the cycle is positive in precisely those cases which we judged to be balanced. This type of reasoning has led Cartwright and Harary to propose the following definition:

DEFINITION. *A graph is* balanced *if every cycle in it is positive.*

We shall prove a basic theorem from Graph Theory which gives us criteria for determining whether a graph is balanced. For the theorem it is convenient to generalize the notion of a path. It will be recalled that a path from p to q was not allowed to go through the same point more than once. If we remove this restriction, we obtain the concept of a *line-sequence* between p and q. If $p = q$, we speak of a *closed line-sequence*, which generalizes the idea of a cycle.

THEOREM 1 (STRUCTURE THEOREM). *The following four conditions are equivalent:*

(1) The graph is balanced.

(2) All closed line-sequences in the graph are positive.

(3) Any two line-sequences between p and q have the same sign.

(4) The set of all points of the graph can be partitioned into two disjoint sets A and B, so that every positive line connects two points in the same set and every negative line connects two points from different sets.

Proof: First we show that *(1)* implies *(2)*. Suppose there are closed line-sequences which are negative. Choose an example with the smallest number of lines possible. This cannot be a cycle, because cycles are positive, by *(1)*. Hence, some point, say p, is crossed more than once. Therefore, we can divide our closed line-sequence into two closed line-sequences, each starting and ending at p. One of these must be negative, and it is shorter than the one we started with, which is a contradiction.

Next we show that *(2)* implies *(3)*. Suppose that two line-sequences between p and q have opposite signs; then the two line-sequences together form a closed line-sequence, which is negative, contrary to *(2)*.

Next we show that *(3)* implies *(4)*. We form A as follows: Take any point and place it into A. If n points have been placed into A, we try to select an additional point such that there is no negative line-sequence between it and any of the previous n points, and add it to A. We continue till no addition is possible. The remaining points are placed in B. Thus all line-sequences between points of A are positive. In particular, so are all lines. It will be sufficient to show that *(i)* a line-sequence between two points r and s of B must be positive, and *(ii)* a line-sequence between p in A and s in B must be negative.

Suppose that a line-sequence between p in A and s in B is positive. Since s could not be added to A, there must be a point q in A such that there is a negative line-sequence between it and s. By *(3)*, q is different from p. But then we can combine the two line-sequences to yield a negative line-sequence between p and q, which is impossible for two points in A. Hence

(ii) follows. On the other hand, if there is a negative line-sequence between r and s in B then we can combine this in a similar manner with a negative line-sequence between some p in A and r to yield a positive line-sequence between p and s—which we now know to be impossible. Hence, (i) follows.

Finally we show that (4) implies (1). Consider any cycle. It can have negative lines on it only when we "cross over" from A to B or from B to A, by (4). Since the cycle must end where it starts, there must be an even number of cross-overs, and hence the cycle is positive.

We have shown that (1) implies (2), which in turn implies (3), which implies (4), which implies (1); hence the four conditions are equivalent.

$$\text{Q.E.D.}$$

This theorem enables us to solve another part of our problem. One natural mathematical formulation of a political organization being compatible with a two-party structure is Condition (4). After all, in the case of a legislative body it states simply that the legislators can be divided into two groups (which we may think of as parties) in such a way that real cooperation is possible only between members of the same group and strong opposition occurs only between members of opposing groups. If we accept this interpretation, then the structure theorem tells us that a legislative body is balanced if and only if it is compatible with a two-party structure.

4. Mathematical treatment of the second problem. Directed graphs serve as mathematical models for a communication network. If x can send a message to y, we include a directed line from x to y. For example, Figure 26 shows a police communication net, where each c is a cop-on-the-beat, d is the dispatcher, r the driver of a radio car, and s the sergeant-at-the-desk, while l is the lieutenant in charge of the unit.

We are interested in developing some measure of the importance of each man in the network, in terms of the fraction of messages that go through

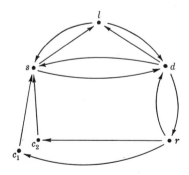

Figure 26

his hands. One simple way of extending this model is to start a message originating from one place—say the lieutenant in Figure 26—and assume that this induces the recipient to send out a message of his own. For lack of any further information we shall assume that he is equally likely to send it to any one of the people whom he can reach. This extends the graph-theory model into a Markov chain model, and we can ask what fraction of the resulting messages passes through each hand in the long run.

The transition matrix for the police network is as follows:

$$
\begin{array}{c@{\quad}c}
 & \begin{array}{cccccc} l & s & d & c_1 & c_2 & r \end{array} \\
\begin{array}{c} l \\ s \\ d \\ c_1 \\ c_2 \\ r \end{array} &
\left(\begin{array}{cccccc}
0 & \frac{1}{2} & \frac{1}{2} & 0 & 0 & 0 \\
\frac{1}{2} & 0 & \frac{1}{2} & 0 & 0 & 0 \\
\frac{1}{3} & \frac{1}{3} & 0 & 0 & 0 & \frac{1}{3} \\
0 & 1 & 0 & 0 & 0 & 0 \\
0 & 1 & 0 & 0 & 0 & 0 \\
0 & 0 & \frac{1}{3} & \frac{1}{3} & \frac{1}{3} & 0
\end{array}\right).
\end{array}
$$

This matrix represents an ergodic chain. This will always be the case, since we assume that a message can be gotten from any person to any other person. Hence the fraction of entries into each state approaches a limit, and this limit is independent of the starting state; it is simply given by the corresponding component of the probability fixed vector of the matrix. Hence, this vector gives us our desired measure of the importance of each person. In the police example, $\alpha = \frac{1}{90}(22, 26, 27, 3, 3, 9)$. Thus our intuition is supported in believing that the dispatcher is most important and the cop-on-the-beat least crucial. Of course, in a full-scale example the differences would be much greater.

Although this measure seems to have intuitively satisfactory properties, it was arrived at in a much less satisfactory manner than the measure of distance in Chapter II. To give full justification to our definition we would have to agree on a set of intuitive conditions, and show that our measure is determined by these.

One such condition would surely be the following: If we can permute the labels of the points of the graph in such a way that the resulting graph is identical with the original one, and if in this permutation a is replaced by b, then a and b should have the same importance in the network. For example, if in Figure 30 we interchange c_1 and c_2, the graph is unchanged (in the sense that the same pairs of points remain adjacent). And we note that c_1 and c_2 were both assigned a measure of importance of $\frac{3}{90}$. Indeed, it is easily seen that this will always be the case. A relabeling of the points of a graph results in a relabeling of the states of the corresponding Markov chain. If after the relabeling the graph remains unchanged, so does the transition matrix, and hence any quantity computed for state a from this matrix must be the same as the corresponding quantity for state b. In particular, the two components of α must be the same.

5. Mathematical treatment of the third problem. The basic relationship here is "x is a superior of y," which we will abbreviate xSy. In our graph-theoretic model each person will again be represented by a point. A (directed) line from x to y will indicate that x is an immediate superior of y. Just as in the last section we represented immediate contact by an arrow and represented each possible communication channel by a (directed) path, here the relationship xSy is represented by having a *directed path from x to $y*.

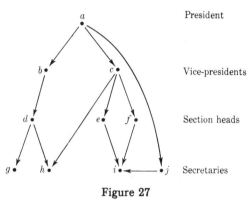

Figure 27

In Figure 27 we represent an organization chart. The president, a, is the superior of all nine other employees. The vice-president b is the superior of d, g, and h. At the other extreme, the secretary j is superior to i, but the other secretaries have no subordinates.

If the relationship xSy is to have the properties that we usually associate with the superior-subordinate relationship, we must require:

(1) No one is his own superior, $\sim(xSx)$.

(2) A person cannot be both the superior and the subordinate of another, $xSy \rightarrow \sim(ySx)$.

(3) A subordinate of a subordinate is a subordinate, $(xSy \ \& \ ySz) \rightarrow xSz$.

THEOREM 2. *The necessary and sufficient condition that the three above requirements hold is that the graph of the organization be free of cycles.*

Proof: Suppose that the graph contains a cycle, say (a,b), (b,c), $\ldots$, (d,e), (e,a). Then by repeated application of (3) we obtain that a is a subordinate of a, which contradicts (1). Hence, if the requirements hold, then the graph is free of cycles. Conversely, suppose that the graph is free of cycles. Then $\sim(xSx)$, since otherwise we have a path from x to x, i.e. a cycle. If we have both xSy and ySx, then we have a path from each to the other.

Combining them yields a closed (directed) line-sequence, and we can use the techniques of the last section to find a cycle. Hence (1) and (2) hold. Next suppose that xSy and ySz, i.e. that we have a path from x to y and from y to z. These two paths cannot cross, since otherwise we would have a cycle. Thus the combination of the two is a path from x to z, and hence (3) holds.

Q.E.D.

So we see that our organization is represented by a directed graph that is free of cycles.

It will be convenient to introduce the concept of the *level* of subordinacy; this is the length of the shortest path from the superior to the subordinate. Thus in Figure 27, j is one level below a, h is two levels below, and g is three levels below the president, while h is also two levels below b.

We wish to develop a measure of the status of each person in the organization. The following are reasonable requirements for the status measure $m(x)$:

(*i*) $m(x)$ is always a whole number.

(*ii*) If x has no subordinates, then $m(x) = 0$.

(*iii*) If, without otherwise changing the structure, we add a new person subordinate to x, then $m(x)$ increases.

(*iv*) If, without otherwise changing the structure, we move a subordinate of x to a lower level (relative to x), then $m(x)$ increases.

A measure of status was proposed by Harary,[†] which we will call $h(x)$: If p has n_k subordinates at level k, then $h(p) = \sum_k k \cdot n_k$. This measure is justified by the following theorem.

THEOREM 3. *If m is any measure satisfying (i) through (iv), then in any organization, for any member x, $m(x) \geq h(x)$. I.e., Harary's measure is the minimal measure satisfying the given requirements.*

The proof of this theorem will be left for a series of exercises (see Exercises 11 and 12).

If we apply the Harary measure to Figure 27, we find

$$m(a) = 1 \cdot 3 + 2 \cdot 5 + 3 \cdot 1 = 16, \quad m(b) = 5, \quad m(c) = 5, \quad m(d) = 2,$$

$$m(e) = 1, \quad m(f) = 1, \quad m(g) = m(h) = m(i) = 0, \quad m(j) = 1.$$

This measure is a good example for showing that a "justification" of the type given does not mean that the measure is perfect. For example, it would be most reasonable to require that

(*v*) If pSq, then $m(p) > m(q)$.

---

† F. Harary, "A Criterion for Unanimity in French's Theory of Social Power," *Studies in Social Power*, ed. D. Cartwright (Ann Arbor, Mich.: Institute for Social Research, 1959), Chap. 10.

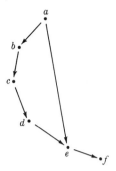

Figure 28

However, in Figure 28 we can see that, although b is a subordinate of a, $m(a) = 9$, and $m(b) = 10$.

This difficulty is easily corrected; we need only modify the definition of "level." Let the number of levels from p to q be the number of lines in the *longest* (rather than shortest) path from p to q. Then the Harary definition will satisfy all five conditions (to be shown in Exercise 13). Under this modified definition, in Figure 28, $m(a) = 15$, $m(b) = 10$.

EXERCISES

1. State which of the following graphs are balanced. If balanced, find the decomposition guaranteed by the Structure Theorem.

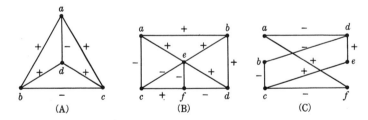

Figure for Exercise 1

2. In the following figure, supply $+$ and $-$ signs to the lines in six different ways, so that the graph is balanced in three cases and not balanced in the other three cases. Verify intuitively that our definition of "balanced" is reasonable.

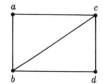

Figure for Exercise 2

3. Prove that a signed graph is balanced if and only if all paths between two given points have the same sign.

4. In the figure of Exercise 2, show that there are five distinct ways of assigning signs so that the resulting signed graph is balanced. (Remember that isomorphic graphs are considered the same.) Interpret each structure.

5. For each of the following communication networks, set up the corresponding transition matrix, and find the importance of each member:

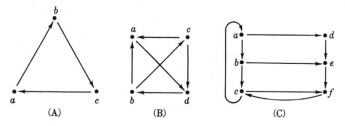

Figure for Exercise 5

6. Set up the transition matrix for the network in Figure 22, and find its probability fixed vector. What is wrong?

7. Check the transition matrix and the vector α given in the text for Figure 26.

8. Find the Harary status measure of each individual in the following organization. Do the same if the definition of "level" is modified (to the length of longest path)

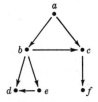

Figure for Exercise 8

9. Mr. x is president of a company with ten employees. How should the company be organized so that x has the largest possible status (i.e. $h(x)$ as large as possible)? When would he have smallest status—assuming that the ten employees must be his subordinates?

10. Find the status measure h of each person in Figure 27, using the modified definition of "level."

11. Verify that the Harary measure h satisfies conditions (i) through (iv).

12. Prove the last theorem of the text as follows: Let $h(x) = n$, and proceed by induction on n.

   (a) Show that if $n = 0$, then $m(x) \geq h(x)$.

   (b) Assume that $m(x) \geq h(x)$ for all x such that $h(x) = k$. Choose an x so that $h(x) = k + 1$. Show that by either moving an employee to one higher level, or by removing an employee, $h(x)$ is reduced to k. Then apply the inductive assumption.

13. Prove that under the modified definition of "level," $h(x)$ satisfies (i) through (v).

14. Prove that in a balanced political structure the two-party division is unique if and only if the graph of the structure is connected.

15. If every cycle in a signed graph has an even number of positive lines, the graph is said to be *antibalanced*. Prove the following structure theorem for an antibalanced graph: A signed graph is antibalanced if and only if its points can be separated into two mutually exclusive subsets, such that each negative line joins two points of the same subset and each positive line joins points from different subsets.

16. A signed graph is *duobalanced* if it is both balanced and antibalanced. Prove the following structure theorem for duobalance: A signed graph is duobalanced if and only if its points can be partitioned into four disjoint subsets A_{11}, A_{12}, A_{21}, A_{22} such that

   (a) There are no lines joining two points of the same subset and no lines joining elements of A_{11} to A_{22} or joining elements of A_{12} to A_{21}.

   (b) All positive lines are A_{11} to A_{21} lines or A_{12} to A_{22} lines.

   (c) All negative lines are A_{11} to A_{12} lines or A_{21} to A_{22} lines.

PROJECT 1

The line-graph of a graph (thought of as a point-graph) is constructed as follows: Each line of the original graph is replaced by a point, and two points in the line-graph are adjacent if the corresponding lines in the original graph have a common point. In a directed graph we form the line-graph similarly by replacing each (directed) line by a point, and we introduce the directed line from l_1 to l_2 (lines of the original graph, points in the line-graph) if l_1 together with l_2 is a path in the original graph, i.e. if l_1 is a line into a point p, and l_2 is a line from the same point p. Thus, for ex-

ample, the line-graph of the directed graph in Figure 22 is given in the
figure below.

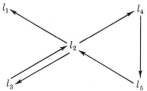

Figure for Project 1

Form the line-graph of the directed graph in Figure 26, and give an
interpretation for it. (*Hint:* There are 12 points and 26 lines in this graph.)
Construct the corresponding transition matrix, and find its probability
fixed vector. Interpret this vector and relate it to the α found in Section 4.

PROJECT 2

Investigate the following definition of status in an organization. Assume
that when an individual receives a command he either carries out the command or passes it on to one of his immediate subordinates. Assume that
the probabilities of these alternatives are all equal. Take as status for p the
mean number of commands generated by an initial command of p before
the command is carried out.

REFERENCES

Harary, F. "A Criterion for Unanimity in French's Theory of Social Power,"
   Studies in Social Power, ed. D. Cartwright. Ann Arbor, Mich.: Institute
   for Social Research, 1959, Chap. 10.

Harary, F., and Cartwright, D. "Structural Balance: A Generalization of
   Heider's Theory," *Psychological Review*, Vol. 63, pp. 277–293.

Harary, F., and Norman, R. Z. "Graph Theory as a Mathematical Model
   in Social Science," Research Center for Group Dynamics Monograph
   No. 2. Ann Arbor, Mich.: Institute for Social Research, 1953.

Harary, F., and Norman, R. Z. *The Theory of Finite Graphs*. Reading, Mass.:
   Addison-Wesley, forthcoming.

Heider, F., "Attitudes and Cognitive Organization," *Journal of Psychology*,
   Vol. 21 (1946), pp. 107–112.

CHAPTER IX

Optimal Scheduling

A Problem in Dynamic Programming

1. The problem. We will consider a general class of optimization problems, and a particular example. We will indicate the method of solution applicable to all such problems and carry it out in detail for the special example.

Let us suppose that a production center wishes to make optimal use of its facilities. This center may be a factory, or a farm, or a small business, or a big industrial cartel. For our purposes we must consider a closed system; that is, one that manufactures all its raw materials. (Or at least we will ignore raw materials supplied from the outside.) We suppose that there are n different materials that enter as raw materials or appear as final products or both.

The center has m different production processes available to it. These may be described by indicating the input and output of each process, for a "unit production." For example, process number i is characterized by the following data: We must supply amounts a_{ij} of good number j, for $j = 1, 2, \ldots, n$, and the process will then produce amounts b_{ij} of good number j, for each j. If we supply twice as much of each raw material, the process will produce twice the output of each good, etc.

In addition to this basic input-output information, we are given two additional pieces of information: We are told just how much is available of each material at the beginning, and we are told the market price of each material. The production is supposed to take place over a fixed period of time, say a month or a year, using the same period for each process.

Our problem is the following: Given the information, and assuming that the market price will not change, how can one best use the available materials and processes to maximize the value of our inventory at the end of a specified number of periods?

To make these problems more specific, let us consider a highly simplified version of a chicken farm. We consider only two kinds of materials, chickens and eggs. (Thus, for example, the cost of feed is neglected.) There are two production processes: hatching of eggs, and laying of eggs. We suppose that any given chicken can hatch four eggs in a given period (e.g. a month), or lay a dozen eggs. Thus hatching has as "input" one chicken and four eggs, and its output is five chickens (including the original chicken!). For laying, our input consists of one chicken, and the output is the one chicken plus a dozen eggs. We suppose that at the beginning we have available 18 chickens and 432 eggs. If chickens cost 30 cents each, and eggs 5 cents, what should we do to maximize the value of our chickens-plus-eggs after four periods?

Let us consider various ways in which this model is oversimplified. For example, we have ignored the fact that chickens normally come in two sexes. We have not allowed for the time delay caused by the fact that a newborn chicken must be given time to grow up before it can be usefully employed. We have not allowed for differences in the productive capacities of various chickens, nor have we allowed for death.

All of these factors could be taken into account in a more complex model, but at the cost of requiring a computing machine to solve the problem. Ignoring the first two factors will simply allow us to build up profits unreasonably fast. This should be taken into account in interpreting the results. The third factor can be incorporated, at least roughly, by thinking of our figures as averages. And the problem of death may be ignored in a sufficiently short production scheme (e.g. 4 months). Thus, although the model is admittedly oversimplified, it incorporates the mathematically significant features of a realistic model.

2. Mathematical formulation. The production processes are represented by two matrices, $A = (a_{ij})$ and $B = (b_{ij})$. These are $m \times n$ matrices. In our chicken farm example,

$$A = \begin{pmatrix} 1 & 4 \\ 1 & 0 \end{pmatrix}; \qquad B = \begin{pmatrix} 5 & 0 \\ 1 & 12 \end{pmatrix}.$$

Hatching is represented by the first row of these matrices. We see that we need 1 chicken and 4 eggs, while the output is 5 chickens and no eggs. Similarly, the second row represents the process of laying.

In addition to this we are given a vector $\mathbf{g} = (g_1, \ldots, g_n)$, which tells us how much we have available of each material, and a price vector

$$\mathbf{p} = \begin{pmatrix} p_1 \\ p_2 \\ \cdot \\ \cdot \\ \cdot \\ p_n \end{pmatrix}.$$

Then $\mathbf{gp}$ = the value of all our goods. In the farm example,

$$\mathbf{g} = (18, 432) \quad \text{and} \quad \mathbf{p} = \begin{pmatrix} 30 \\ 5 \end{pmatrix}.$$

The value of our original stock is $\mathbf{gp} = 2700$ (or \$27).

Let us suppose that in a given period we decide on an activity schedule and procedure. This may be represented by $t = (t_1, t_2, \ldots, t_m)$, where t_i indicates the number of units of production by process i. In our example t_i must be an integer, but this is not always the case. There is no reason why the number of tons of steel manufactured should be an integer. It is convenient to allow t to be any real-valued vector. Even in the integer-valued case, in a practical problem the numbers are likely to be large enough so that rounding t off in the solution should make no significant difference, and the computations would become much simpler. In any reasonable example, a solution that calls for fractional values should be nearly optimal when rounded off.

Suppose then that activities are carried out according to schedule t. Then the vector tA, which has n components, tells us our raw-material needs. Since these cannot exceed the available supply, we have:

RESTRICTION: $0 \leq t$, *and* $tA \leq g$.

By a vector inequality we require that the inequality hold for all components. For our example, if $t = (t_1, t_2)$ and $g = (C, E)$, we have

$$0 \leq t_1, \quad 0 \leq t_2, \quad t_1 + t_2 \leq C, \quad \text{and} \quad 4t_1 \leq E.$$

Geometrically this means that the values of t_1 and t_2 must lie inside the area T in Figure 29.

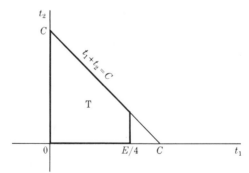

Figure 29

We started with amounts g. We used up amounts tA. The output of the various amounts is given by tB. Hence at the end of the period we have

$$g' = g - tA + tB = g + t(B - A).$$

Our profit during the period is clearly $t(B - A)p$. Thus, the vector $(B - A)p$ is the "profit vector," giving the profit attained in carrying out unit production under the various processes. If any component of this vector is negative, then this particular process loses us money. In our example

$$B - A = \begin{pmatrix} 4 & -4 \\ 0 & 12 \end{pmatrix}; \qquad (B - A)\mathbf{p} = \begin{pmatrix} 100 \\ 60 \end{pmatrix}.$$

Thus both activities are profitable, but using a chicken for hatching is more profitable than for laying.

3. The method of solution. We shall employ a method developed by R. Bellman. He has shown that this method is useful for a wide variety of different types of dynamic programming problems.

Let us introduce the "value functions," $v_k(\mathbf{g})$ = the value of our inventory after k periods if we start with the amounts $\mathbf{g}$ and proceed optimally. (All values are computed relative to the fixed price vector $\mathbf{p}$.) Now let us suppose that we know the function v_k. How would we compute v_{k+1}? We start with amounts $\mathbf{g}$; if we adopt the production schedule $\mathbf{t}$ for the first period, then we have the amounts $\mathbf{g}' = \mathbf{g} + \mathbf{t}(B - A)$ available at the end of the period, and there are k periods left to us. If for the remaining periods we act optimally, then our final value will be $v_k(\mathbf{g}')$—by the definition of v_k. Thus our problem for the first period is simply the following:

(★)   *Choice of optimal procedure:* Choose $\mathbf{t}$ so that $v_k(\mathbf{g} + \mathbf{t}(B - A))$ is a maximum, subject to the restrictions $0 \leq \mathbf{t}$ and $\mathbf{t}A \leq \mathbf{g}$. Hence $v_{k+1}(\mathbf{g})$ is the maximum value thus obtained. To start us off, we have $v_0(\mathbf{g}) = \mathbf{g}\mathbf{p}$. (I.e., the value of $\mathbf{g}$, if we have zero time left, is the immediate market value.)

This procedure has reduced the many-period problem to several separate one-period problems. We use v_0 to compute both the optimal procedure for one period and v_1. Then we can use v_1 to compute both the optimal procedure for the first of two periods and v_2. We use this to find both the optimal procedure for the first of three periods and v_3, etc.

However, we must pay a price for this simplification. To compute $v_{k+1}(\mathbf{g})$ we need to know $v_k(\mathbf{g}')$, and we don't know what $\mathbf{g}'$ is until our problem is solved. Hence we will need to know the values of $v_k(\mathbf{g})$ for all possible $\mathbf{g}$, and not just for our special initial $\mathbf{g}$.

We may summarize this procedure as follows: We compute the optimal procedure for k periods and $v_k(\mathbf{g})$, for all $\mathbf{g}$, step by step. If we already know the optimal procedure for k periods and v_k, then (★) gives us v_{k+1} and the optimal procedure for the first one of the $k + 1$ periods, in terms of v_k. The optimal procedure for the remaining k of the $k + 1$ periods is the optimal k-period procedure for $v_k(\mathbf{g}')$ when $\mathbf{g}'$ represents the initial amounts available.

Thus if we wish to solve a four-period problem, we can solve this in four (increasingly difficult, but manageable) steps for all conceivable $\mathbf{g}$. Actually, it suffices to find the general solution and $v_k(\mathbf{g})$ for all $\mathbf{g}$ for $k = 1, 2, 3$. For

$k = 4$ we can restrict ourselves to our special $\mathbf{g}$ values. This will be the method illustrated in the next section.

There are various other tricks for simplifying a computation. For example, the solution cannot depend on the units in which various quantities are measured. This often enables us to work with simpler numbers. In the chicken farm example, we may, for instance, use a nickel as a unit of money instead of a penny. Then $\mathbf{p} = \begin{pmatrix} 6 \\ 1 \end{pmatrix}$. We will indeed use this unit, for simplicity. Again, if we multiply the vector $\mathbf{g}$ by a number, this simply multiplies our various quantities, such as $\mathbf{t}(B - A)$, $\mathbf{g}'$, and $v_k(\mathbf{g})$, by the same number; hence, the optimal procedure is unchanged. Thus the optimal procedure can depend only on the ratios of quantities, in our example simply on C/E.

4. Solution of the chicken farm problem. Let us first introduce an additional simplification, which is made possible by a special feature of our problem. If $\mathbf{g} = (C,E)$ gives the number of chickens and eggs available at the beginning of any period, and $\mathbf{t} = (t_1,t_2)$ is our production schedule, then t_1 is the number of chickens used for hatching and t_2 the number used for laying. In the light of this, the restriction $t_1 + t_2 \leq C$, which was derived above, simply says that we cannot use more chickens than we have. But it is obvious that there is never a reason why a chicken should be idle. Hence we let $t_1 = t$, and $t_2 = C - t$, to assure that $t_1 + t_2 = C$. Thus $\mathbf{t} = (t, C - t)$.

Our remaining three restrictions then take on the form $0 \leq t, t \leq C$, and $t \leq E/4$. The first two have obvious meanings, and the last assures that we do not hatch more eggs than we have available. We compute that $\mathbf{t}(B - A) = (4t, 12C - 16t)$. Further, instead of writing $v_k(\mathbf{g})$, where $\mathbf{g} = (C,E)$, we simply write $v_k(C,E)$. Thus ($\star$) takes the form:

($\star\star$) Choose optimal procedure t so that $v_k(C + 4t, E + 12C - 16t)$ is a maximum, subject to the restrictions $0 \leq t$, $t \leq C$, and $t \leq E/4$. Then $v_{k+1}(C,E)$ is the maximum value thus obtained.

To start us off, we have $v_0(C,E) = 6C + E$.

We begin by letting $k = 0$ in ($\star\star$). Then we must choose t, subject to the restrictions, so as to maximize

$$v_0(C + 4t, E + 12C - 16t) = 18C + E + 8t.$$

Since t occurs with a positive coefficient, it is to our advantage to maximize t and so to have as many chickens hatching as possible. But t can be no greater than the smaller of C and $E/4$, due to our restrictions. We thus have two cases:

CASE 1. $C \leq E/4$ or $C/E \leq \frac{1}{4}$. Then we choose $t = C$. (All chickens are hatching.)

$$v_1 = 26C + E, \text{ the maximum we obtain for } v_0.$$

CASE 2. $C/E \geq \frac{1}{4}$. Then we choose $t = E/4$. (Hatch all eggs.)

$$v_1 = 18C + 3E.$$

We have included the borderline case $C/E = \frac{1}{4}$ twice, since then $t = C = E/4$; hence the two formulas for v_1 should give the same answer. Indeed, they yield the common value $(15/2)E$.

Now let $k = 1$ in (★★). We have found that

$$v_1(C,E) = \begin{cases} 26C + E & \text{if } C/E \leq \frac{1}{4}, \\ 18C + 3E & \text{if } C/E \geq \frac{1}{4}. \end{cases}$$

Therefore,

$$v_1(C + 4t, E + 12C - 16t) = \begin{cases} 38C + E + 88t & \text{if } 32t \leq E + 8C, \\ 54C + 3E + 24t & \text{if } 32t \geq E + 8C. \end{cases}$$

We obtained the "if" conditions by simplifying $(C + 4t)/(E + 12C - 16t) \leq \frac{1}{4}$, and $\geq \frac{1}{4}$, respectively.

We again note that in either case it is to our advantage to maximize t. Hence we may introduce Cases 1, 2 as before, where in the first case $t = C$, and in the second $t = E/4$. This will determine our optimal procedure for the first period of the two, but to determine what the optimal strategy is for the second period, and to find v_2, we must also consider whether in the resulting output $C'/E' \leq \frac{1}{4}$. Thus we shall number the four possible cases 11, 12, 21, 22. For example, Case 12 is the case where originally $C/E \leq \frac{1}{4}$, and hence in the first period $t = C$, all chickens hatch. But as a result, $C'/E' \geq \frac{1}{4}$, and hence we must employ Case 2 strategy for the second period, i.e. $t = E'/4$, and use the second formula for v_1. We know that the condition for this is $32t \geq E + 8C$, and $t = C$, and hence that $32C \geq E + 8C$, or $C/E \geq \frac{1}{24}$. So, Case 12 occurs when $\frac{1}{24} \leq C/E \leq \frac{1}{4}$, and then $v_2 = 78C + 3E$ (which is obtained from the second formula for v_1 by letting t equal its optimal value C).

The other cases may be treated similarly. We summarize the results:

CASE	CONDITION	$v_2(C,E)$ (unit = 5¢)	OPTIMAL PROCEDURE FOR	
			FIRST PERIOD	SECOND PERIOD
11	$C/E \leq \frac{1}{24}$	$126C + E$	all chickens hatch	all chickens hatch
12	$\frac{1}{24} \leq C/E \leq \frac{1}{4}$	$78C + 3E$	all chickens hatch	hatch all eggs
22	$\frac{1}{4} \leq C/E \leq \frac{7}{8}$	$54C + 9E$	hatch all eggs	hatch all eggs
21	$\frac{7}{8} \leq C/E$	$38C + 23E$	hatch all eggs	all chickens hatch

Table 1

Now let $k = 2$ in (★★). From Table 1 we obtain the following values for $v_2(C + 4t, E + 12C - 16t)$:

11: $138C + E + 488t$ if $t \leq (\frac{1}{112})E - (\frac{3}{28})C$,

12: $114C + 3E + 264t$ if $(\frac{1}{112})E - (\frac{3}{28})C \leq t \leq \frac{1}{32}E + \frac{1}{4}C$,

22: $162C + 9E + 72t$ if $\frac{1}{32}E + \frac{1}{4}C \leq t \leq \frac{7}{144}E + \frac{19}{36}C$,

21: $314C + 23E - 216t$ if $\frac{7}{144}E + \frac{19}{36}C \leq t$.

In the first three cases it is to our advantage to maximize t; in the last case we want to minimize it. Thus if t is below $(\frac{7}{144})E + (\frac{19}{36})C$, then it should be maximized, which means that we set t equal to C, or $E/4$, whichever is smaller. Otherwise we want it to equal $(\frac{7}{144})E + (\frac{19}{36})C$. More simply, this means that we set t equal to C, or $E/4$, or $(\frac{7}{144})E + (\frac{19}{36})C$, whichever is smallest. We shall refer to these as Cases 1, 2, and 3.

From the above description we see that Cases 1 and 2 may be combined with 11, 12, or 22 above, yielding six possible strategy patterns for the three periods. Actually, when we check the conditions for 211, we find that they are never fulfilled, thus there are only five such cases. A sixth case is, however, obtained in the combination 321. Since in this case t is minimized, we are on the borderline of 21 and 22 above; hence 321 may equally be described as 322.

The six possible patterns are summarized in Table 2. We shall illustrate the computations by working out 112. Since it involves using Procedure 1 for the first period, $t = C$, and the result must yield 12 above. Hence

$$(\frac{1}{112})E - (\frac{3}{28})C \leq C \leq (\frac{1}{32})E + \frac{1}{4}C.$$

Thus $(\frac{1}{122})E \leq (\frac{31}{28})C$, and $(\frac{3}{4})C \leq (\frac{1}{32})E$; or $(\frac{1}{24}) \leq C/E \leq (\frac{1}{24})$. Substituting $t = C$ in the formula 12 above we obtain $378C + 3E$ as our value for $v_3(C,E)$.

We have now found the general solution patterns for three periods. We may use the results in Table 2 to solve our specific four-period problem. We have 18 chickens and 432 eggs to start with; hence $C < E/4$. Thus the bounds on t are $0 \leq t \leq 18$. We must compute $v_3(C + 4t, E + 12C - 16t)$, and then we have to decide which choice of t maximizes this quantity. As we have noted before, if t occurs with a positive coefficient, then we choose the maximum value ($t = 18$), and if it occurs with a negative coefficient, then we choose the minimum ($t = 0$). Of course the formula will change from case to case, and hence we have to work it out in all six cases.

Thus, in Case 111, $626(C+4t) + (E+12C-16t) = E + 638C + 2488t$; this shows us that t occurs with a positive coefficient. We also obtain a positive coefficient in the next four cases; only in Case 212 is the coefficient negative. What is the possible maximum for C'/E'? Since t is at most 18, $C' = C + 4t \leq 90$. Similarly, $E' = E + 12C - 16t \geq 360$. Therefore,

$C'/E' \leq \frac{1}{4}$, and so Case 212 cannot result from the given initial values of C and E. Hence we must choose $t = 18$.

Case	Condition	$v_3(C,E)$ (unit $= 5\cancel{c}$)	Optimal Procedure for		
			First Period	Second Period	Third Period
111	$C/E \leq \frac{1}{124}$	$626C + E$	all chickens hatch	all chickens hatch	all chickens hatch
112	$\frac{1}{124} \leq C/E \leq \frac{1}{24}$	$378C + 3E$	all chickens hatch	all chickens hatch	hatch all eggs
122	$\frac{1}{24} \leq C/E \leq \frac{7}{68}$	$234C + 9E$	all chickens hatch	hatch all eggs	hatch all eggs
321 322	$\frac{7}{68} \leq C/E \leq {}^{29}\!/_{76}$	$200C + 12\frac{1}{2}E$	compromise: $({}^{19}\!/_{36}C + \frac{7}{144}E)$ chickens hatch	hatch all eggs	all chickens hatch *and* all eggs are hatched
222	${}^{29}\!/_{76} \leq C/E \leq \frac{7}{8}$	$162C + 27E$	hatch all eggs	hatch all eggs	hatch all eggs
212	$\frac{7}{8} \leq C/E$	$114C + 69E$	hatch all eggs	all chickens hatch	hatch all eggs

Three types of procedure:

1. "All chickens hatch." Use all chickens for hatching. Some eggs are normally left over.

2. "Hatch all eggs." Use enough chickens to hatch all available eggs. Left-over chickens lay eggs.

3. "Compromise." Some chickens hatch, some lay, and some eggs are left. Proportion of hatchers to layers is precisely determined.

Table 2

Thus $t = 18$, $C' = 90$, $E' = 360$, and we have Case 321 for the next three periods. Thus our complete production schedule is as in Table 3.

Thus we have obtained our optimal schedule. It enables us to increase an initial investment of 540 units ($27) to 22,500 units ($1125) in four periods.

5. Interpretation of results. The most noticeable feature of the solution is the very high profit ratio (the value of final inventory divided by the value of initial inventory), which is clearly unrealistic. However, that was caused by oversimplifications in the model. For example, if we had built into the model a delay, to allow for the time it takes chickens to grow into hens, the profit rate would have been much more modest.

PERIOD NUMBER	PROCEDURE	CASE	C	E	VALUE (unit = 5¢)
0	The given initial state		18	432	540
1	18 C's hatch	1	90	360	900
2	65 hatch, 25 lay	3	350	400	2500
3	100 hatch, 250 lay	2	750	3000	7500
4	750 C's hatch	1 or 2	3750	0	22500

Table 3

Let us instead concentrate on some general features of the solution. We note that the schedule in Table 3 is quite complicated. It could certainly not have been "guessed," nor is it likely that someone would arrive at it by trial and error in a reasonable length of time. Thus, dynamic programming provides a useful and practical device for solving economic problems.

Although the solution could not have been guessed; once it is found, certain features of it can be made intuitively plausible. We note in Table 3 that in the last two periods we triple our investment, but in the first two periods we do less well. It is easily seen that the best we can ever hope to do in any one period is to triple the value of the available raw materials, since each production process triples the value of the materials used. (Hatching requires 10 units investment and produces 30 units, while laying requires only 6 units and produces 18.) Thus we triple our investment if all available materials are used. Since all chickens are always used, this means that the maximum rate is achieved under Case 2, when all eggs are hatched. It should be observed that in five of the cases in Table 2 this is achieved for the last period. The exception is Case 111 where chickens are so scarce that even if all the activity in all periods consists of hatching some eggs are left over.

To continue this analysis, we note that in the last four cases in Table 2 we succeed in hatching all eggs in at least two of the three periods. The exception is 112, where we have enough chickens to get all eggs hatched at the end, but this cannot be achieved sooner. The 321 case is particularly interesting. Here the "compromise" in Period 1 is so set up that the optimal procedure of hatching all eggs is feasible in the remaining periods, and we end up with every egg hatched at the end. (See Table 3.)

An equally interesting case is 222. Here Activity 2 is possible in every period, and hence we triple our investment in every period. Our original investment, worth $6C + E$ units, is expanded to $162C + 27E$ by the end, which is a factor of $27 = 3^3$. Thus, in order to achieve the highest possible profit ratio, we must start with a number of chickens that is between $29\!\!\!/_{76}$ and $7\!\!\!/_8$ of the number of eggs, or somewhere between 38 and 87 per cent. This gives us considerable freedom in choosing an "ideal" initial inventory.

EXERCISES

Exercises 1 through 6 refer to the chicken farm example developed in the text.

1. Suppose that we have one chicken and 40 eggs available. What is the optimal procedure for three periods of production? Use Table 2, and work out a complete schedule similar to Table 3. What is the profit ratio?

2. Suppose that we have 20 chickens and 40 eggs available. Work out the schedule for an optimum procedure for three periods. What is the profit ratio?

3. Suppose that we have 10 chickens and 100 eggs available. Work out the optimal schedule for *four* periods.

4. Suppose that we have 36 chickens and 144 eggs. Work out the optimal production schedule for *four* periods.

5. What is the largest possible profit ratio for four periods? Find the bounds within which C/E must lie for this ratio to be achievable.

6. Prove that if $C/E = 1\!\!\!/_2$, then it is possible to achieve a profit ratio of 3^n in n periods, for any number n. Describe the optimal pattern.

Exercises 7 through 15 refer to a modification of the chicken farm example: It is assumed that each chicken can hatch 5 eggs in one period, or lay 15 eggs. The price of chickens is 28¢ and of eggs 4¢.

7. Set up A, B, and $\mathbf{p}$ (in convenient units).

8. If $\mathbf{g} = (C,E)$, and we adopt a schedule of $\mathbf{t} = (t, C - t)$, compute $\mathbf{g}'$, the available materials for the next period.

9. What are the restrictions on t?

10. Modify $(\bigstar\bigstar)$ to be applicable to this problem.

11. Find the optimal procedures for each case of a one-period problem, and compute $v_1(C,E)$.

12. Find the optimal procedures for each case of a two-period problem, and compute $v_2(C,E)$.

13. Find the optimal schedule for two periods if we have (a) 10 chickens and 10 eggs, (b) 1 chicken and 10 eggs, (c) 1 chicken and 35 eggs.

14. For what C/E value(s) is the profit ratio greatest in a two-period problem?

15. Find the optimal schedule for a *three*-period problem if $C = 7$, $E = 35$.

PROJECT

A certain industry has two production processes available: The first process uses up one unit of material A and two units of material B; the output is two units of A. The second process uses one unit of A and three units of B, and the output is eight units of B. The current market price is 20¢ for a unit of A and 5¢ for a unit of B.

How must the procedure of the present chapter be modified to be applicable to this problem? (*Hint:* Most of what we did is still applicable, but not all of it.) Work out the general solution pattern for three periods. How can 10 dollars be best invested in raw materials to produce a maximum return over three periods?

Try to generalize your results to n time periods.

REFERENCE

Bellman, Richard. *Dynamic programming*. Princeton, N. J.: Princeton University Press, 1957.

Appendixes

A Fixed Point Theorem

DEFINITION 1. *By Euclidean m-space, denoted by E_m, we mean the set of all vectors of the form* $\mathbf{x} = (x_1, x_2, \ldots, x_m)$ *where the components x_j are real numbers, and if* $\mathbf{x} = (x_1, x_2, \ldots, x_m)$ *and* $\mathbf{y} = (y_1, y_2, \ldots, y_m)$ *are any two points in E_m, then the* distance between $\mathbf{x}$ and $\mathbf{y}$, *denoted by $d(\mathbf{x},\mathbf{y})$ is defined to be*

$$d(\mathbf{x},\mathbf{y}) = \sqrt{(x_1 - y_1)^2 + (x_2 - y_2)^2 + \cdots + (x_m - y_m)^2}.$$

In one, two, and three dimensions this is the familiar notion of distance on the line, in the plane, and in space.

DEFINITION 2. *A subset of A of E_m is* bounded *if there exists a number K such that $d(\mathbf{x},\mathbf{y}) < K$ for every pair $\mathbf{x},\mathbf{y}$ in A.*

DEFINITION 3. *A subset A of E_m is* convex *if whenever $\mathbf{x}$ and $\mathbf{y}$ are in A so are all points of the form $t\mathbf{x} + (1 - t)\mathbf{y}$, for numbers t such that $0 \leq t \leq 1$.*

A set then is convex if it has the property that whenever two points are in the set so is every point which lies on the line-segment connecting the two points. For example, the solid sphere in three dimensions is a convex set, but its surface is not.

DEFINITION 4. *Let $\mathbf{x}_n$, $n = 1, 2, \ldots$, be a sequence of points in E_m, and $\mathbf{x}$ also be a point in E_m. We say that $\mathbf{x}_n$* approaches $\mathbf{x}$ as n tends to infinity, *written $\mathbf{x}_n \to \mathbf{x}$, if $d(\mathbf{x}_n,\mathbf{x}) \to 0$ as n tends to infinity.*

DEFINITION 5. *A subset A of E_m is* closed *if whenever $\mathbf{x}_n$, $n = 1, 2, \ldots$, is a sequence of points in A such that $\mathbf{x}_n \to \mathbf{x}$, then $\mathbf{x}$ is also in A.*

The solid sphere in three dimensions is closed, but if we remove the surface this is no longer the case.

THEOREM 1. *If $\{\mathbf{x}_n\}$ is any sequence of points in a closed bounded subset of E_m, then there is a point $\mathbf{x}$ in this set and a subsequence $\{\mathbf{x}_{n_j}\}$ of $\{\mathbf{x}_n\}$, such that $\mathbf{x}_{n_j} \to \mathbf{x}$.*

DEFINITION 6. *A mapping T of A into B is* continuous *if whenever $\mathbf{x}_n \to \mathbf{x}$ with $\mathbf{x}_n$ and $\mathbf{x}$ in A, it follows that $T\mathbf{x}_n \to T\mathbf{x}$.*

An example of a continuous mapping of the sphere into itself is obtained by rotating the sphere around an axis, by some specified degree.

THEOREM 2. BROUWER FIXED POINT THEOREM. *Any continuous mapping of a closed convex bounded subset of E_m into itself has at least one fixed point. That is, there is a point $\mathbf{x}$ such that $T\mathbf{x} = \mathbf{x}$.*

The proof of this theorem in general is quite difficult. However, in E_1 the proof is simple and illuminating. A closed bounded convex subset of E_1 is a closed interval $[a,b]$. A continuous mapping of this interval into itself means that we have a function with domain $[a,b]$ and range a subset of $[a,b]$, which is continuous. Let f be this function. It is sufficient to show that the function g defined by $g(x) = f(x) - x$ is 0 for some x in $[a,b]$. But since $f(a) \geq a$ and $f(b) \leq b$ we see that $g(a) \geq 0$ and $g(b) \leq 0$. If either $g(a) = 0$ *or* $g(b) = 0$, then the theorem is proved. If not, it follows from a familiar theorem in the calculus that a continuous function cannot go from above the axis to below the axis without crossing the axis.

An interesting application of the fixed point theorem in m dimensions is the following: Let P be the transition matrix of a Markov chain. (See Appendix C.) Let A be the set of all probability vectors, i.e. vectors with non-negative components and sum of components equal to 1. Then A is easily seen to be closed, convex, and bounded. Consider the transformation $\mathbf{y} = \mathbf{x}P$. This takes points of A into points of A and is continuous. Hence there is at least one probability vector $\boldsymbol{\alpha}$ such that $\boldsymbol{\alpha}P = \boldsymbol{\alpha}$. In the case of an ergodic chain this vector is unique and gives the average number of times in each of the states, in the long run. In an absorbing chain it need not be unique. In fact, a vector which is 1 for a component corresponding to an absorbing state and 0 for all others is a fixed probability vector for P.

APPENDIX B

Utility Functions

An individual is confronted with certain choices concerning combinations of n goods. A *utility function* u is designed to indicate by a single number the amount of satisfaction such a combination provides for him. Thus, if he is offered amounts $x_1, \ldots, x_n$ of the goods, $u(x_1, \ldots, x_n)$ is a numerical measure of his satisfaction. We shall give a brief summary of the theory of utility functions for the case of two goods. The theory for more than two goods is quite similar. The reader not familiar with functions of two variables is advised to read this appendix in conjunction with Appendix F.

Such measures are by necessity quite arbitrary. However, one normally uses them only to compare alternative sets of goods (known as *commodity bundles*), to determine which one is preferred. Thus only the ordering of u values is relevant, and hence u may always be replaced by $\phi(u)$, where ϕ is a monotone increasing function.

Even under these circumstances, utility functions represent an idealized situation, since we assign a value to all conceivable combinations, whether such combinations may be realized in practice or not. We are therefore asking the individual to specify his preferences in complete detail. But this fiction is a convenient one for many economic problems. Let us investigate what conditions one would wish to impose on u for it to be a reasonable utility function.

First of all, small changes in the quantities of goods should not have very drastic effects on u. This means that u changes smoothly in its various arguments, which is at the very least a requirement of continuity. However, it is more convenient to assume that u is not only continuous but that all its second partial derivatives exist. Can we say anything about these derivatives?

First of all, let us consider the first (partial) derivatives. Since we are considering the case of only two arguments, we shall write the arguments as x and y, and the value of our utility function as $u(x,y)$. It is immediately clear that u_x cannot be negative; if the amount of the first good given us is increased, without changing the amount of the second good, how can the satisfaction diminish? We shall actually make the stronger assumption that

(1) $u_x > 0$ and $u_y > 0$ for all arguments.

Since the first partial derivative u_y is positive, for a given x there can be at most one y yielding a fixed value of u. Thus $u(x,y) = c$ determines $y = f(x)$, y as a function of x, for all those values x which make $u = c$ possible. The graphs of these functions are known as *indifference curves*, since along a given curve the choice of goods is a matter of indifference. These curves contain all the qualitative information that u yields. The fact that the first derivatives are positive assures that the indifference curves with higher u values lie above the lower ones.

Next, we shall differentiate the function $u(x,f(x))$. For this we use the analogue of the "chain-rule" for functions of two variables, which states that the derivative of $u(g(x),f(x))$ is $u_x g' + u_x f'$. Since $u(x,f(x)) = c$, its derivative must be 0:

$$(2) \qquad u_x + u_y f' = 0, \quad \text{hence} \quad f' = -u_x/u_y < 0.$$

Thus f is monotone decreasing.

There is no condition directly applicable to the second partial derivatives of u, but we shall derive two restrictions on combinations of partial derivatives. Let us consider the function u_x along a given indifference curve, i.e., the values $u_x(x,f(x))$ as a function of x. These measure the marginal increase in satisfaction if for fixed utility $u = c$ an amount of good x is added. The more we already have of the good—for fixed utility—the less the marginal increase should be. That is, $u_x(x,f(x))$ should be a monotone decreasing function of x. In terms of the derivative this states:

$$(3) \qquad u_{xx} + u_{xy} f' < 0.$$

On the other hand, u_y should increase with x, along a given indifference curve. That is, the function $u_y(x,f(x))$ is monotone increasing in x:

$$(4) \qquad u_{yx} + u_{yy} f' > 0.$$

Now we can compute f''. This is the derivative of $-u_x(x,f(x))/u_y(x,f(x))$; hence:

$$(5) \qquad f'' = \frac{(-u_{xx} - u_{xy} f')u_y + u_x(u_{yx} + u_{yy} f')}{u_y{}^2}.$$

And from (1), (3), and (4) we see that $f'' > 0$. Hence the function f is monotone decreasing and "concave upwards," and thus a family of indifference curves looks as in Figure 30.

Since decisions based on u should remain unchanged when u is replaced by $\phi(u)$, we must check that our various results are not altered by such a change. Since we want to have partial derivatives of the second order for u, we assume that ϕ has two derivatives, and since ϕ is to be monotone increasing, $\phi' > 0$.

First of all, the indifference curves are unaltered, since if $u = c$, then $\phi(u) = \phi(c)$. (Simply the "labels" on the curves are changed.)

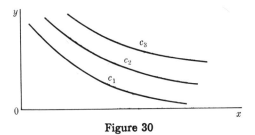

Figure 30

The partial derivative of $\phi(u)$ with respect to x is $\phi'(u) \cdot u_x$, and with respect to y it is $\phi'(u) \cdot u_y$. Both of these are clearly positive, and so, (1) holds. Furthermore, when we form their ratio, ϕ' cancels, and hence (2) holds. Quite similar computations show that (3), (4), and (5) are modified only by factors of ϕ'; in the two inequalities these do not affect the sign, and in (5) they cancel.

We shall now illustrate these results in terms of the utility function $u(x,y) = x^2 y$. First we compute

$$u_x = 2xy, \quad u_y = x^2, \quad u_{xx} = 2y, \quad u_{xy} = u_{yx} = 2x, \quad u_{yy} = 0.$$

If $u = x^2 y = c$, then $y = c/x^2$; hence $f(x) = c/x^2$. Therefore,

$$f'(x) = -2c/x^3, \quad \text{and} \quad f''(x) = 6c/x^4.$$

We can easily verify that (1) through (5) hold.

Let us now replace u by $\log u$. We obtain the new utility function $2 \log x + \log y$, and for this (taken as u),

$$u_x = 2/x, \quad u_y = 1/y, \quad u_{xx} = -2/x^2, \quad u_{xy} = u_{yx} = 0, \quad u_{yy} = -1/y^2,$$

and $u = \log c$ yields the curve previously identified as $u = c$. We can again verify that our conditions hold, and that the expressions for f, f' and f'' are unchanged. However, we note that the signs of the second derivatives have changed. Thus a condition placed directly on one of the second partial derivatives would not have been legitimate.

Finite Markov Chains

A *Markov chain* is a mathematical model for describing a certain type of process that moves in a sequence of steps through a set of states. In a finite Markov chain we have a finite number of states, which we denote by $s_1, s_2, \ldots, s_r$. When the process is in state s_i there is probability p_{ij} that the next position will be state s_j. The matrix $P = (p_{ij})$ is called the *transition matrix*. Its entries are non-negative and its rows have sum 1. To specify the process completely, we must give P and the starting state.

Matrix operations play a basic role in this theory. For example, the probability of moving from state s_i to s_j in n steps is given by the ijth entry of P^n. And if $\boldsymbol{\pi}$ is a row vector whose components give the probability of being in the various states at the present moment, $\boldsymbol{\pi}P$ gives the probabilities after one step, and $\boldsymbol{\pi}P^n$ after n steps.

The study of the general finite Markov chain can be reduced to the study of two special types of chains. If a set of states *communicate* with each other, i.e., the process can move from any state to any other, and if the set cannot be left, then these states form an *ergodic chain*. If, on the other hand, there is a set of states from which the process can "escape," then we may study these states as part of an *absorbing chain*.

Absorbing chains. A state is *absorbing* if, once entered, it cannot be left. A chain is an *absorbing chain* if it has at least one absorbing state and if, from every state, it is possible (not necessarily in one step) to reach an absorbing state.

EXAMPLE (RANDOM WALK). We take as states the integers 1, 2, 3, 4, 5. We assume that when in States 2, 3, or 4, the process moves one unit to the right with probability $\frac{2}{3}$ and one unit to the left with probability $\frac{1}{3}$. When it reaches 1 or 5 it remains in this state. The transition matrix for this chain is

$$
P = \begin{array}{c} 1 \\ 2 \\ 3 \\ 4 \\ 5 \end{array}
\begin{pmatrix}
1 & 0 & 0 & 0 & 0 \\
\frac{1}{3} & 0 & \frac{2}{3} & 0 & 0 \\
0 & \frac{1}{3} & 0 & \frac{2}{3} & 0 \\
0 & 0 & \frac{1}{3} & 0 & \frac{2}{3} \\
0 & 0 & 0 & 0 & 1
\end{pmatrix}.
$$

In studying absorbing chains it is convenient to put the transition matrix in canonical form. We do this by listing the absorbing states first. We then partition the transition matrix as follows:

$$P = \begin{array}{c} \\ \text{absorbing} \\ \text{nonabsorbing} \end{array} \overset{\begin{array}{cc} \text{absorbing} & \text{nonabsorbing} \end{array}}{\left(\begin{array}{c|c} I & O \\ \hline R & Q \end{array} \right)}.$$

Here I is the identity matrix (has 1's on the main diagonal and 0's elsewhere), and O is a matrix of zeros. These correspond to the fact that once an absorbing state is entered the chain stays there, and to the fact that from an absorbing chain one cannot enter a nonabsorbing state, respectively. Q and R are non-negative matrices representing transition probabilities from nonabsorbing states. Since P has row sums equal to 1, and R cannot be identically O, Q has row sums ≤ 1, and at least one row has a sum less than 1. It is this feature that distinguishes a set which can be left from an ergodic set of states.

The basic result about finite absorbing chains is that the process is sure to reach an absorbing state. Hence Q^n tends to O. Even more important is the fact that the infinite series $N = I + Q + Q^2 + \cdots$ always converges (in each entry), and that the limit is the inverse of the matrix $I - Q$, i.e., $N = (I - Q)^{-1}$. The matrix N is called the *fundamental matrix* of the chain. We shall also use the following quantities:

1 is a column vector all of whose components are 1.

τ is the vector giving the row sums of N. This equals $N\mathbf{1}$.

n_{ij} is the mean number of times in state s_j when the chain is started in state s_i. (s_i and s_j are nonabsorbing states.) This is the ijth entry of N.

t_i is the mean number of steps before absorption, if the chain is started in state s_j. This is the ith entry of τ.

b_{ik} is the probability starting in the nonabsorbing state s_i that the process is absorbed in the absorbing state s_k. This is the ikth entry of the matrix $B = NR$.

EXAMPLE CONTINUED. Putting our "random walk" example into canonical form we have

$$P = \begin{array}{c} \\ 1 \\ 5 \\ 2 \\ 3 \\ 4 \end{array} \overset{\begin{array}{ccccc} 1 & 5 & 2 & 3 & 4 \end{array}}{\left(\begin{array}{cc|ccc} 1 & 0 & 0 & 0 & 0 \\ 0 & 1 & 0 & 0 & 0 \\ \hline \frac{1}{3} & 0 & 0 & \frac{2}{3} & 0 \\ 0 & 0 & \frac{1}{3} & 0 & \frac{2}{3} \\ 0 & \frac{2}{3} & 0 & \frac{1}{3} & 0 \end{array} \right)}.$$

The fundamental matrix is

$$N = (I - Q)^{-1} = \begin{pmatrix} 1 & -\frac{2}{3} & 0 \\ -\frac{1}{3} & 1 & -\frac{2}{3} \\ 0 & -\frac{1}{3} & 1 \end{pmatrix}^{-1} = \begin{pmatrix} \frac{7}{5} & \frac{6}{5} & \frac{4}{5} \\ \frac{3}{5} & \frac{9}{5} & \frac{6}{5} \\ \frac{1}{5} & \frac{3}{5} & \frac{7}{5} \end{pmatrix}.$$

From this we obtain our descriptive quantities

$$\tau = N\mathbf{1} = \begin{pmatrix} \frac{7}{5} & \frac{6}{5} & \frac{4}{5} \\ \frac{3}{5} & \frac{9}{5} & \frac{6}{5} \\ \frac{1}{5} & \frac{3}{5} & \frac{7}{5} \end{pmatrix}\begin{pmatrix} 1 \\ 1 \\ 1 \end{pmatrix} = \begin{pmatrix} \frac{17}{5} \\ \frac{18}{5} \\ \frac{11}{5} \end{pmatrix}$$

$$B = NR = \begin{pmatrix} \frac{7}{5} & \frac{6}{5} & \frac{4}{5} \\ \frac{3}{5} & \frac{9}{5} & \frac{6}{5} \\ \frac{1}{5} & \frac{3}{5} & \frac{7}{5} \end{pmatrix}\begin{pmatrix} \frac{1}{3} & 0 \\ 0 & 0 \\ 0 & \frac{2}{3} \end{pmatrix} = \begin{pmatrix} \frac{7}{15} & \frac{8}{15} \\ \frac{1}{5} & \frac{4}{5} \\ \frac{1}{15} & \frac{14}{15} \end{pmatrix}.$$

The fact that B has row sums equal to one follows from the general fact that in an absorbing Markov chain the process will with probability one reach an absorbing state.

Ergodic chains. An *ergodic chain* is a chain such that it is possible to go between any two states (not necessarily in one step). An important special case of an ergodic chain, called a *regular chain*, is a chain such that for some n, P^n has no zero entries. That is, it is possible to go between any two states in n steps. For example, if $p_{ii} > 0$ for some i, then P is regular.

EXAMPLE. As reported in our *Introduction to Finite Mathematics*,[†] in the Land of Oz there are three kinds of weather: rain, nice, and snow. If they have a nice day they are just as likely to have snow as rain on the next day. If they have snow (or rain) they have an even chance of having the same the next day. If there is a change from snow or rain, only half of the time is this a change to a nice day. We form a three-state Markov chain with states R, N, and S for rain, nice, and snow, respectively. The resulting chain is regular and its transition matrix is

$$P = \begin{array}{c} \\ R \\ N \\ S \end{array}\begin{array}{c} \begin{array}{ccc} R & N & S \end{array} \\ \begin{pmatrix} \frac{1}{2} & \frac{1}{4} & \frac{1}{4} \\ \frac{1}{2} & 0 & \frac{1}{2} \\ \frac{1}{4} & \frac{1}{4} & \frac{1}{2} \end{pmatrix} \end{array}.$$

A basic result in the study of ergodic chains is that

$$\lim_{n \to \infty} \frac{P + P^2 + \cdots + P^n}{n} = A,$$

where A is a matrix with each row the same vector $\boldsymbol{\alpha} = (a_1, a_2, \ldots, a_r)$. The vector $\boldsymbol{\alpha}$ has all components positive and is the unique vector with

† Englewood Cliffs, N. J.: Prentice-Hall, 1959.

components adding up to 1 such that $\alpha P = \alpha$. For regular chains this limit may be strengthened to $\lim_{n\to\infty} P^n = A$. In this case the probability $p_{ij}^{(n)}$ of going from i to j in a large number of steps is essentially independent of the starting state. In either case, a_j gives the fraction of the times that the process can be expected to be in each of the states in the long run. We may write $A = \mathbf{1}\alpha$; hence for any row vector $\boldsymbol{\pi}$, $\boldsymbol{\pi}A = (\boldsymbol{\pi}\mathbf{1})\alpha$. In particular, $\alpha A = \alpha$. Thus in a regular chain $\boldsymbol{\pi}P^n$ tends to $(\boldsymbol{\pi}\mathbf{1})\alpha$, a multiple of the vector α. Only the proportionality constant, $\boldsymbol{\pi}\mathbf{1} = \sum_j \pi_j$, depends on $\boldsymbol{\pi}$.

The *fundamental matrix* of an ergodic chain is

$$Z = (I - P + A)^{-1}.$$

For a regular chain,

$$Z = I + \sum_{n=1}^{\infty} (P^n - A).$$

It is easily seen that $\alpha Z = \alpha$ and $Z\mathbf{1} = \mathbf{1}$. We may think of α as representing an equilibrium distribution, which the chain approaches no matter how it is started. The matrix Z measures the "total deviation from equilibrium" during the history of the chain.

EXAMPLE CONTINUED. In the Land of Oz example we must find a vector $\alpha = (a_1, a_2, a_3)$ such that

$$(a_1, a_2, a_3) \begin{pmatrix} \frac{1}{2} & \frac{1}{4} & \frac{1}{4} \\ \frac{1}{2} & 0 & \frac{1}{2} \\ \frac{1}{4} & \frac{1}{4} & \frac{1}{2} \end{pmatrix} = (a_1, a_2, a_3)$$

$$a_1 + a_2 + a_3 = 1.$$

This leads to four equations in three unknowns. These equations have the unique solution $\alpha = (\frac{2}{5}, \frac{1}{5}, \frac{2}{5})$. Hence we can expect in the long run $\frac{2}{5}$ of the days to be rainy, $\frac{1}{5}$ nice, and $\frac{2}{5}$ snowy.

We treat in Chapter VII a Markov chain which has an infinite number of states. The states are in fact the non-negative integers. The theory of such chains is considerably more complicated than in the finite case. Many of the results for finite chains do not hold for infinite chains. For example, if an absorbing chain is defined in the same manner as for the finite case, it is not always true that the chain must reach an absorbing state with probability one. In Chapter VII we see examples where in fact the absorption probability is less than one.

REFERENCES

Kemeny, John G., and others. *Finite Mathematical Structures*. Englewood Cliffs, N. J.: Prentice-Hall, 1958.

Kemeny, John G., and Snell, J. Laurie. *Finite Markov Chains*. Princeton, N. J.: D. Van Nostrand Co., 1960.

APPENDIX D

Generating Functions

DEFINITION. *Let w_0, w_1, ... be a sequence of numbers. If*

$$W(s) = w_0 + w_1 s + w_2 s^2 + \cdots$$

converges in some interval $-s_1 < s < s_0$, then $W(s)$ is called the generating function *for the sequence $\{w_j\}$.*

Let U be a possibility space. Let f be a function on this space whose range consists of non-negative integers. Let $u_j = \mathbf{Pr}\,[f = j]$. Then the generating function of f is the generating function for the sequence $\{u_j\}$, that is,

$$U(s) = \sum_j u_j s^j.$$

Note that $U(1) = 1$, and the generating function converges at least for $-1 \leq s \leq 1$. We can also associate with f the *tail generating function* $V(s)$ as the generating function for the sequence $\{v_j\}$ with $v_j = \mathbf{Pr}\,[f > j]$.

Theorem 1. *For $-1 < s < 1$, $V(s) = \dfrac{1 - U(s)}{1 - s}$.*

$V(1)$ exists if and only if $U'(1)$ exists, and either of these conditions is equivalent to the finiteness of the mean of f. Indeed, in this case

$$\mathbf{M}[f] = U'(1) = V(1).$$

Even if the mean is finite, the variance may still be infinite. To assure the finiteness of the variance we must further require that $V'(1)$, or equivalently $U''(1)$, should exist. In this case

$$\mathbf{Var}\,[f] = U''(1) + U'(1) - U'(1)^2$$
$$= 2V'(1) + V(1) - V(1)^2.$$

Assume now that f and g are two independent functions defined on a possibility space U, with non-negative integer values. Let $a_j = \mathbf{Pr}\,[f = j]$ and $b_j = \mathbf{Pr}\,[g = j]$. Let $c_j = \mathbf{Pr}\,[(f + g) = j]$. Then

$$c_j = a_0 b_j + a_1 b_{j-1} + \cdots + a_j b_0.$$

THEOREM 2. *If f and g are independent functions with generating functions $A(s)$ and $B(s)$, then the function $f + g$ has generating function $C(s) = A(s)B(s)$.*

In particular, if $h_n = f_1 + f_2 + \cdots + f_n$ is the sum of n independent functions each having the same generating function $A(s)$, then h_n has the generating function $A(s)^n$.

THEOREM 3. *Assume that $f_1, f_2, \ldots$ are independent functions each having the same generating function $A(s)$. Let N be a function independent of the f_j's, having generating function $N(s)$. Then the generating function for the function*

$$h_N = f_1 + f_2 + \cdots + f_N$$

is

$$B(s) = N(A(s)).$$

A Combinatorial Lemma

In this appendix we present the solution to a counting problem which is needed for Chapter VII.

The problem that we consider is one of counting the number of possible tree diagrams of a specified kind. A *tree diagram* is a diagram of the type indicated in Figure 31. Points like A, B, C, D, and E are called *branch points*.

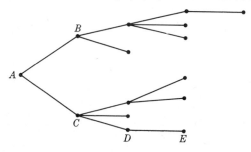

Figure 31

We are interested, for example, in the number of tree diagrams that have a specified number of branch points. All possible trees having five branch points are shown in Figure 32. We note that there are fourteen such trees.

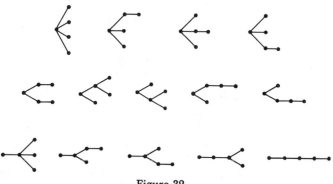

Figure 32

In addition to this problem we shall also need the solution of a more specific problem. A branch point is said to be of *type* k if k branches emit from this point. For example, for the tree diagram of Figure 31, points A and B are of Type 2, C is of Type 3, D of Type 1, and E of Type 0. We denote by $\alpha(n; \nu_0, \nu_1, \ldots, \nu_n)$ the number of trees which have n branch points of which ν_0 are of Type 0, ν_1 of Type 1, etc. For example, we see that $\alpha(5; 2, 2, 1) = 6$. The six graphs counted are shown in Figure 33.

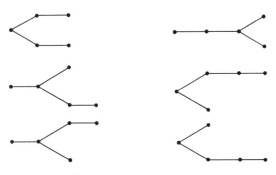

Figure 33

We shall prove that in general $\alpha(n; \nu_0, \nu_1, \ldots, \nu_n) = \left(\dfrac{1}{n}\right)\left(\dfrac{n}{\nu_0, \ldots, \nu_n}\right)$ and the total number of trees with n branch points is $\left(\dfrac{1}{n}\right)\left(\dfrac{2n-2}{n-1}\right)$. Note that according to these formulas

$$\alpha(5; 2, 2, 1) = \tfrac{1}{5}\left(\frac{5}{2, 2, 1}\right) = \frac{1}{5}\left(\frac{5!}{2!\,2!\,1!}\right) = 6,$$

and the total number of trees having five branch points is

$$\tfrac{1}{5}\left(\frac{8}{4}\right) = 14.$$

First of all we note the following restriction on the possible arguments of α (*cf.* (5) in Chapter VII):

(1)   For any tree, $\displaystyle\sum_{k=1}^{n} \nu_k = n$ and $\displaystyle\sum_{k=1}^{n} k\nu_k = n - 1.$

The former expresses that there are exactly n branch points, and the latter expresses that the number of branches is $n - 1$ (a fact characteristic of trees).

LEMMA. *Under restriction* (1),

$$\alpha(n; \nu_0, \ldots, \nu_n) = \frac{1}{n} \binom{n}{\nu_0, \ldots, \nu_n},$$

and the sum of these α's for fixed n is $\frac{1}{n} \binom{2n-2}{n-1}$.

Proof: We shall order the branch points of the tree. We start with the branch point furthest to the left, and then move to the right, working upwards at each level. Let us represent one such tree as an ordered n-tuple $\langle n_1, n_2, \ldots, n_n \rangle$, where the number k occurs ν_k times in the n-tuple. Here n_i is the number of branches of the ith branch point. Every possible tree is represented uniquely by such an n-tuple, but not every n-tuple is possible. For example, $n_1 = 0$ is impossible for $n > 1$. We will show the following result: If we consider the cyclic permutations of an n-tuple of the given kind, the n permutations are all distinct, and exactly one of the n cyclic permutations represents a tree.

From this result the lemma will follow easily. The total number of ordered n-tuples in which k occurs ν_k times is $\binom{n}{\nu_0, \ldots, \nu_n}$, and $1/n$ of these represent trees. To find the second formula of the lemma, we may argue as follows. The sum of the numbers $n_1 + n_2 + \cdots + n_n = n - 1$. Hence we are interested in the number of ways that $n - 1$ can be written as an ordered sum of n terms. But this is well known to be $\binom{2n-2}{n-1}$. (See *Introduction to Finite Mathematics*, p. 105, Exercise 15.) And $1/n$ of these represent trees.

We must now show of the cyclic permutations of a given n-tuple that (A) all n permutations are distinct, (B) one of them represents a tree, (C) only one can be a tree. For this purpose we must have a usable criterion of when the n-tuple represents a tree. There are the conditions (1) that the numbers must satisfy, but for a given n-tuple this simply means that $n_1 + n_2 + \cdots + n_n = n - 1$. We will show that a given ordering of these numbers represents a tree if and only if

$$(2) \qquad n_1 + n_2 + \cdots + n_i \geq i \quad \text{for } i = 1, \ldots, n - 1.$$

Originally we have one "path" open in the tree. If $n_i = 0$, then a previous path closes; and if $n_i > 1$, then new paths are opened. Specifically, the number of paths is increased by $n_i - 1$. Hence the number of paths still open after the branches of the ith branch point is $1 + (n_1 + \cdots + n_i - i)$. Our condition (2) therefore asserts that some path must be kept open till the end. We also see that (1) asserts that all paths are closed at the end.

Let us first prove (C). Suppose $\langle n_1, \ldots, n_n \rangle$ satisfies (2). Consider the cyclic permutation $\langle n_{k+1}, \ldots, n_n, n_1, \ldots, n_k \rangle$. By hypothesis,

$n_1 + \cdots + n_k \geq k$, and $n_1 + \cdots + n_n = n - 1$. Hence $n_{k+1} + \cdots + n_n \leq n - 1 - k < n - k$. Hence the second n-tuple violates (2).

Next we shall prove (B). Suppose that $<n_1, \ldots, n_n>$ violates (2). Let k_1 be the first place so that $n_1 + \cdots + n_{k_1} < k_1$. Consider the tail of the n-tuple. If this still violates (2), then let k_2 be the first place such that $n_{k_1+1} + \cdots + n_{k_2} < k_2 - k_1$. And so on. Say we arrive at $k_1, k_2, \ldots, k_m$ in this way, and that the segment following n_{k_m} satisfies (2). Then each of the m segments has a sum one less than the number of elements in the segment, and hence the tail we are left with must have a sum $m - 1$ greater than the number of elements in it. If we move this tail up to the front, then $< n_{k_m+1}, \ldots, n_n, n_1, \ldots, n_{k_m} >$ satisfies (2). This is easily seen, since a violation can only occur at the end of one of the m segments, and the new initial segment compensates for $m - 1$ of these. Hence the sum (2) is less than the number of elements only at the end.

An example will illustrate this method: $<2, 1, 0, 0, 1, 0, 2, 2, 0>$ satisfies (1), but violates (2). $k_1 = 4$, $k_2 = 6$—that is, we have segments with four and two elements at the beginning, and a tail of three elements. When we rotate this to the front, we obtain $<2, 2, 0, 2, 1, 0, 0, 1, 0>$, which satisfies (2).

Finally, we must show (A). Suppose that a cyclic permutation carried one of our n-tuples into an identical one. Call this permutation P_1, and we have $P_1 x = x$, where x is an n-tuple. By (B) we know that there is a cyclic permutation P_2 such that $P_2 x$ satisfies (2). But $P_1 P_2 x = P_2 P_1 x = P_2 x$, since cyclic permutations commute, and hence $P_1 P_2 x$ satisfies (2). This is possible according to (C) only if P_1 is the identity transformation.

Q.E.D.

APPENDIX F

Functions of Two Variables

Most of the book deals with functions f of one variable x, but occasionally we have to consider a function g of several variables x_1, x_2, ..., x_n. Such functions are defined analogously to a function of one variable. Given a number x, f assigns a value $f(x)$ to this argument; similarly, given numbers x_1, x_2, ..., x_n, g assigns a value $g(x_1, x_2, ..., x_n)$ to the set of arguments. Geometrically viewed, f assigns a numerical value to each point on a line, whereas g assigns a number to each point in n-dimensional space. Many of the techniques applicable to functions of one variable can be extended to functions of more than one variable. We shall illustrate this in terms of functions $f(x,y)$ of two variables.

First of all, we can compute *partial derivatives*, which measure rates of change parallel to an axis. For example, f_x is the rate of change of the function f parallel to the x-axis, i.e., the derivative of f computed by holding y constant. If we have a formula for $f(x,y)$, we can find a formula for $f_x(x,y)$ by simply carrying out an ordinary differentiation with respect to x in which we pretend that y is a constant. The partial derivative f_y is defined similarly.

For example, if $f(x,y) = x^2 e^{3y}$, then $f_x(x,y) = 2x e^{3y}$ and $f_y(x,y) = 3x^2 e^{3y}$. At the point $(1,0)$ we thus find $f(1,0) = 1$, $f_x(1,0) = 2$, and $f_y(1,0) = 3$.

As another example we consider $f(x,y) = p/(px + qy + r)$, where p, q, r are given constants. We compute $f_x(x,y) = -p^2/(px + qy + r)^2$ and $f_y(x,y) = -pq/(px + qy + r)^2$. Hence, at the point $(1,1)$, $f(1,1) = p/(p + q + r)$, $f_x(1,1) = -p^2/(p + q + r)^2$, and $f_y(1,1) = -pq/(p + q + r)^2$.

Taylor's Theorem for a function of one variable states that a sufficiently smooth function may be approximated very closely by a polynomial, and it asserts that the polynomial of degree n best approximating the function near $x = a$ (in a well-defined sense) is $f(a + u) = \sum_{k=0}^{n} (1/k!) f^{(k)}(a) \cdot u^k$, where $f^{(k)}$ is the kth derivative of f and u is a small number. There is a similar theorem for functions of more than one variable, approximating such a function by a polynomial in the variables $u_i = (x_i - a_i)$ near the point $(a_1, a_2, ..., a_n)$. We shall be interested only in linear approximations, that is, approximations by a first-degree polynomial.

If f is sufficiently smooth near the point (a,b)—it will suffice to assume that it has continuous second derivatives near the point—then we may approximate f as follows: Let $x = a + u$, $y = b + v$, where u and v are small, and then

$$f(x,y) = f(a + u, b + v) \approx f(a,b) + u \cdot f_x(a,b) + v \cdot f_y(a,b).$$

The error in this approximation is bounded by $Au^2 + Buv + Cv^2$ in a given neighborhood of the point, for fixed numbers A, B, C. Hence by making u and v small enough, we can make the error-term negligible.

Let us, for example, approximate $x^2 e^{3y}$ near $(1,0)$. We then obtain for $x = 1 + u$ and $y = v$, $x^2 e^{3y} \approx 1 + 2u + 3v$. If $|u| < .1$ and $|v| < .1$, it can be shown that the error is bounded by $3u^2 + 9uv + 15v^2$; hence if $|u| < \epsilon$ and $|v| < \epsilon$, the error is less than $27\epsilon^2$, which is 27ϵ times ϵ, and 27ϵ will be very small if ϵ is very small. Thus the contribution of the error can be made negligible in comparison with the contributions of $2u$ and of $3v$. It is this type of reasoning that justifies neglecting quadratic terms in u and v if we are interested only in the behavior of f near the given point.

For our other example, letting $x = 1 + u$ and $y = 1 + v$ we obtain near $(1,1)$

$$p/(px + qy + r) \approx p/(p + q + r) - p^2 u/(p + q + r)^2 - pqv/(p + q + r)^2.$$

We can also define higher order partial derivatives: f_{xx} is the partial derivative of the function f_x with respect to x, f_{xy} the partial derivative of f_x with respect to y, and f_{yx} and f_{yy} are the two partial derivatives of f_y. For example, in our first example we find $f_{xx} = 2e^{3y}$, $f_{xy} = 6xe^{3y} = f_{yx}$, and $f_{yy} = 9x^2 e^{3y}$. We note that $f_{xy} = f_{yx}$, which will always be the case if they are continuous.

Index

Index

143